Emerging Strategies for Supporting Student Learning

Emerging Strategies for Supporting Student Learning

Barbara Allan

facet
publishing

Published by Facet Publishing
7 Ridgmount Street, London WC1E 7AE
www.facetpublishing.co.uk

Facet Publishing is wholly owned by CILIP: the Chartered
Institute of Library and Information Professionals.

British Library Cataloguing in Publication Data
A catalogue record for this book is available from the British
Library.

ISBN 978-1-78330-070-9 (paperback)
ISBN 978-1-78330-107-2 (hardback)
ISBN 978-1-78330-146-1 (e-book)

First published 2016

Text printed on FSC accredited material.

Typeset from author's files in 10/13 pt Revival 565 and
Frutiger by Flagholme Publishing Services
Printed and made in Great Britain by CPI Group (UK) Ltd,
Croydon, CR0 4YY.

Contents

Figures and tables

Acknowledgements

I would like to thank all the library and information workers who have had an input to this book. This may have been through their participation in workshops delivered at CILIP and other organizations, or through their publications, websites and blogs.

Special mention must be made of the Librarians' Information Literacy Annual Conference (LILAC) 2015, which provided great insights into the many innovative practices currently taking place worldwide in contemporary academic libraries.

I would especially like to thank staff and students at the University of Westminster and the University of Hull who have influenced this work and shared their practices with me. In particular, I thank everyone involved in the innovative Learning Futures programme at the University of Westminster, as they have provided inspiration for some of the ideas contained in this book.

An earlier book of mine helped to inform this one: *The No-Nonsense Guide to Training in Libraries* (Facet Publishing, 2013). Writing this new book has been an interesting learning experience as we are undergoing such a rapid period of change with new ideas about working with students, learning and teaching, and the use of new technologies such as social media. At times, I have felt as if approaches to supporting students' learning were changing as I was writing about them. This book very much captures the current situation and I imagine that it will continue to rapidly change and develop.

Finally, thank you to Denis and Sarah, who have been patient and supportive during my time working on this book.

Barbara Allan

1

Introduction

Introduction to the book

The aim of this book is to enable library and information workers to provide support to students in higher education. It is relevant to different groups working in colleges and universities, including: library and information workers, staff developers, educational technologists, educational development project workers, and educational change agents, as well as students of librarianship who are planning their careers in higher education institutions.

Anyone who works in higher education, either in a university or college, will know that we are experiencing rapid change and that it is a turbulent environment. Change factors that affect everyone include globalization, rapidly changing technologies, political instability, terrorism and environmental issues. As outlined later in this chapter, universities and colleges are positioned in a changing environment and this is requiring new approaches to supporting student learning.

This book gives an introduction to the current landscape of higher education, the very diverse nature of students in colleges and universities today, as well as changing ideas about learning and teaching. It explores different ways of providing support for students, e.g. in developing their information and digital literacy, and through face-to-face, online and blended learning courses and other forms of support.

Emerging Strategies for Supporting Student Learning is a straightforward and accessible guide to learning and teaching practices appropriate for use with higher education students and it covers a wide range of tools and techniques (relevant to face-to-face and online practices), which will suit different groups of students in different contexts. Library and information workers are involved in supporting very different groups of students, e.g. they might work with large groups of 500+ students or deliver specialist programmes to very small groups of research students. Some library staff are working in contexts where resources are tightly squeezed and there appear to be few opportunities for innovation. In contrast, many universities and colleges are investing heavily in their support systems and structures for students, and this brings great opportunities for change and innovation.

Finally, the nature and speed of the changes that are being experienced within colleges and universities means that the need for continuous professional development (CPD) is vital. Individual library and information workers now have many different opportunities to keep up to date and maintain their professional development so that they can continue to meet the needs of students and their career aspirations.

Introduction to this chapter

Higher education institutions are experiencing rapid change as they develop new ways of managing the current turbulent environment and prepare for an uncertain future in an increasingly complex and connected global environment. It is both an exciting and challenging time. Examples of changes affecting higher education include:

- changing student expectations
- changing student populations
- increased focus on student employability
- increased demand for a flexible curricula
- changing information technologies particularly social media
- changes in pedagogies
- changing employer expectations
- changing relationships with knowledge
- a rise in interdisciplinary working
- government interventions
- resource issues – changes in student funding
- increased regulation and legislation
- increased competition from local and global competitors
- unintended consequences (as a result of grappling with multiple changes).

One of the responses to this complex environment is the production of a plethora of reports and papers which highlight the potential way forward for higher education. A number of key themes have emerged including:

- the new learning landscape
- student expectations and experiences
- flexible learning
- new learning spaces
- employability
- internationalization.

These are the themes which form the focus of this chapter and this provides an introduction to the current context of library and information work in higher education.

As a result of these changes and new priorities, colleges and universities are implementing change programmes and this is briefly explored along with a number of case studies in the section on responses to change. Alongside these institutional changes, library and information workers are working in new and different ways, and often with new working partnerships. The section titled 'Changing ways of working for library and information professionals' completes this overview of the current context for librarians working in higher education and supporting students. The final section of this chapter gives an introduction to the structure of this book and subsequent chapters.

Changing the learning landscape

The learning landscape within colleges and universities has changed from a rather static situation to an environment where there are many new and different kinds of learning spaces and students and staff are working and collaborating together in many different ways. Institutions vary hugely as some have embraced these changes while others are still in 'catch-up' mode and working out how to support their students in this new environment.

There is an extensive literature on the theme and one initiative which is having a major influence on practice in the UK is a project called Changing the Learning Landscape (Leadership Foundation for Higher Education, 2014). This was funded by the Higher Education Funding Council for England (HEFCE) and it aimed to equip university leaders in the strategic use of learning and digital technologies, in order to support learning, teaching and the student experience. The report from this project provides a glimpse into the direction of travel for many institutions and considers success from a learning, student, staff and institutional perspective. These findings are summarized below as they help to give an overview of the many changes which are taking place in higher education institutions.

These are the changes to learning and teaching identified in the report:

- Students are actively engaged and involved in the design of innovative learning programmes and assessment tasks.
- Students experiment with new technologies and digital media.
- Students are able to use online submission and feedback systems, and obtain timely and effective personal feedback.
- Staff support flipped classrooms (see Chapter 8) and conversational approaches to learning.
- Students have access to instant feedback in classrooms and real-time online collaboration.

- Students have access to appropriate tools and technologies for learning and career development.

The impact of these changes on library and information practices are explored from Chapter 3 onwards.

These are the changes for students identified in the report:

- Students are confident in their use of technology for both learning and engaging with the university.
- Student champions are used to support their peers in the use of technology enhanced learning.
- Digital literacy is embedded within the curriculum.
- The student voice strongly influences the student experience.
- There is seamless access to online systems for learning, career development and administration.
- Students who need additional support are identified through the use of analytics.
- There is more flexibility over modes of study, e.g. full time and part time.
- There is greater use of technology to promote more blended learning and distance learning.

The very diverse nature of the student body is explored in Chapter 2 and digital literacy is discussed in Chapter 3. Chapters 5–10 consider the process of designing and implementing courses (online, blended and face to face) to support student learning.

These are the changes for university staff identified in the report:

- Staff achieve minimum standards of digital and information technology literacies.
- Staff are confident in their integration of technology into their teaching and support for student learning.
- Staff have access to CPD to improve their confidence in technology enhanced learning.
- There are increased interactions with students as staff move away from traditional offices into new learning spaces.
- There are more approaches to learning and teaching through engagement with communities of practice, which are facilitated through online collaboration and action research facilitated by e-learning.
- Staff are skilled in designing for online learning as well as face-to-face learning and teaching experiences.

The final chapter considers the importance of keeping up to date and presents a range of approaches with a particular emphasis on digital skills and social media. Institutional level changes identified in the report include:

- Governors and senior managers understand the digital environment.
- The academic delivery model incorporates blended learning, which enables lecturers to spend more time working one-to-one with students.
- Academic workload models support flexible learning (face to face, blended and online).
- Digital literacies are embedded within the institution and its strategic plans.
- Student learning spaces change to support more informal learning and networking.
- Institutions provide a robust technical infrastructure including wifi and 4G coverage.
- Information systems support technology enhanced learning and assessment.

The subject of institutional strategy and change are beyond the scope of this book.

Student expectations and experiences

The previous section highlighted the changing technological and digital landscape of higher education. Students entering higher education come from diverse backgrounds and have had a huge range of prior educational experiences. The diversity of the student body is considered in Chapter 2. In this chapter, the diversity of their technological backgrounds, expectations and experiences are considered based on research carried out as part of a Jisc (Joint Information Systems Committee) programme.

Beetham and White (2013) carried out research into students' expectations and experiences in the digital environment. They found that many new students are unsure about the use of technology in supporting learning and wider academic life. Each year, new students from very different technological backgrounds arrive at college or university, from those whose previous educational experience was at the cutting edge of technology to others who have had limited exposure to it. Students may not be clear about how to combine or integrate their personal devices with those of the institution, and they may have little experience of adhering to institutional policies and practices relating to technologies. As they gain experience within higher education their perceptions of and attitudes towards the digital environment are likely to change and develop.

Students expect to experience a sophisticated and seamless digital environment which has the following characteristics (Beetham and White, 2013, 4):

- digital technologies integrated into their courses and used for learning, teaching and assessment

- consistent and clearly guided use of the virtual learning environment for administrative and teaching purposes
- ubiquitous access to the web and to wifi on campus and in student residences
- ability to connect their devices to the university's network
- explicit support and training in using information systems and specialist technologies relevant to their courses
- academic staff who have relevant and up-to-date digital skills
- help desk support for all their technology needs including those related to their own devices
- access to a range of flexible learning spaces, and a digital infrastructure
- access to institutional information technology (IT) particularly desktop computers and printers
- access to reliable and detailed information about their (prospective) course of study
- access to reliable and up-to-date course-related information
- personal updates (e.g. timetable) via their mobile or tablet devices
- an institutional e-mail address.

Beetham and White (2013) also explored students' experiences with technology on entry to higher education and they found it to be extremely diverse both on entry and within the same course over time. They demonstrated that 'we can say with some confidence that the ICT [information and communication technology] capability and know-how of teaching staff has the strongest positive impact on students' experience of using digital technologies for study'. In addition, they found the following:

- Students are largely ignorant of the range of services, software and support available to them at university.
- Students are so used to seamless access they do not understand when they are crossing boundaries, e.g. between institutionally-paid-for to free-on-the open-web services.
- Students rarely use technology for advanced knowledge-related activities or problem solving unless they have been required to do so by their course or tutor.
- Students want more guidance on academically credible sources and academically legitimate uses of online content.
- Students are familiar with aps [sic], not applications. Academic software and specialist systems require structured introduction in the context of meaningful tasks.
- Students place a high value on experience with work-place technologies and research-like digital practices.
- Students learn important and valuable digital practices from other students.

(Beetham and White, 2013, 4)

This research demonstrates the importance of ensuring that students understand the digital landscape that they will experience within the university and that they are prepared for their future digital work environment. This involves a proactive approach and the embedding of digital literacy within their courses and in their wider university life, which requires different professional groups (academics, library and information workers, IT staff, careers staff and others) to work together. In addition, it demonstrates the importance of peer learning and students learning from each other.

Flexible learning

Implicit in the concept of changing the learning landscape, outlined earlier, is the idea of flexible learning. Flexible learning is often described in terms of flexibility with respect to pace, place and mode (e.g. McLinden, 2013). This is illustrated in Table 1.1.

Table 1.1 *The characteristics of flexible learning*	
Characteristics	**Examples**
Pace	Part time, full time, mixed part time and full time, accelerated, decelerated, flexible pace
Place	Physical location – in the higher education institution, work-based, at home, while travelling (at home or abroad)
Mode	Face to face, blended learning, online learning, distance learning, distance teaching

Increasingly, flexible learning is associated with and mediated through the use of technology and Gordon (2014) considers the use of technology enhanced learning to support flexible learning, identifying the following technologies:

- computer-based/-assisted/-aided learning/training: these forms of teaching emphasise the use of a computer as the platform for delivery and may be intended to educate or train depending on the focus of the material
- courseware: a form of computer-based learning, typically learning materials delivered through a computer
- m-learning: a form of e-learning where the delivery platform is a mobile device, e.g. a laptop, smartphone or tablet
- virtual learning environments: portals to provide access to learning support, including course information, communication (forums, messaging, announcements), course content (lecture notes and sources), and assessment and feedback
- immersive learning environments: models (typically 3D) where participants can explore and learn in a simulated environment or virtual world
- computer-based assessment/e-assessment: utilizing computer technology to assess students. These can incorporate multiple-choice testing, parsing of language or comparison of symbolic (mathematical) expressions. They may be diagnostic, formative or summative

- open learning: sharing of learning resources through open licensing and agreements, e.g. massive open online courses (MOOCs)
- collaborative technologies: Web 2.0 offers community and user involvement that maps well onto many learning activities.

(Gordon, 2014, 8)

Flexible learning is very relevant to the work of library and information workers who are increasingly engaging with the very many different forms of technology enhanced learning identified by Gordon (2014) and using them to provide a flexible service to students who are increasingly able to choose the pace, place and mode of study.

Library spaces

Wilson (2015), writing from an architectural perspective, gives a useful summary of the importance of focusing on students when designing libraries:

> A 21st century library provides diverse learning experiences. Printed and digital information are combined in an environment that is user-focused and service-rich. Students can work collaboratively in spaces that support today's social and learning patterns. Because resources can be accessed from anywhere, spaces need the flexibility to be used for impromptu study sessions or classes by both students and teachers. . . . **The library can also play an important role in supporting social learning.** Incorporating large-scale active learning spaces, and social learning areas in larger, flexible spaces, encourages peer-to-peer learning, which extend learning beyond the classroom environment. Other social learning spaces outside classrooms and in other areas of the campus become an extension of the library as a study space and demonstrate a shift in the definition of the traditional learning and research library.
>
> (Wilson, 2015)

Today, many libraries in colleges and universities are providing extremely diverse spaces either within or beyond the library walls, for example:

- quiet study spaces
- group learning spaces
- social learning spaces
- teaching spaces
- spaces for staff development
- informal learning spaces, e.g. cafés, rest spaces and snooze centres.

These changes are taking place in the development of new libraries and within traditional library buildings which are being redesigned and refitted. In addition, new learning spaces outside the library buildings are being developed for use by students and these often give access to support from library and information workers. The following two examples illustrate the types of changes currently taking place. Further examples may be found at the following website: www.designinglibraries.org.uk/.

Case study: University of Michigan's Taubman Health Sciences Library with no books

Freed (2015) writes about the University of Michigan's new Taubman Health Sciences Library. The new building is designed to encourage students to work collaboratively with their peers and students from other programmes. Books have been moved off site as most of them are available as e-books and hard copies may be requested. The building contains new collaborative classrooms with mobile furniture, and all surfaces (including tables and walls) can be written on using white board markers. The library also contains study rooms of various sizes, and there is space for socializing including a student lounge, restricted by key card access, which features comfortable chairs and large plasma TV screens.

Further information including images is available at www.mlive.com/news/ann-arbor/index.ssf/2015/08/university_of_michigan_unveils_2.html.

Case study: Brynmor Jones Library, University of Hull

The University of Hull's website (www2.hull.ac.uk/lli/redevelopment/index.html) announces the redevelopment of its library as follows:

Following its £28 million redevelopment, completed early in 2015, the Brynmor Jones Library is now a state-of-the-art place of learning for generations to come.

Bring your online life with you. Our high-speed wireless network will let you use your mobile device wherever you go in the BJL. We have 350 open access PCs, 48 borrowable laptops, multifunction printers, scanners and photocopiers, and self-service issuing facilities in all area. Do what you need to do, wherever you are in the building.

Teaching and learning spaces are modern and flexible. Silent study? Innovative teaching? Group projects? However you would like to work, there is a space for you, with access to all our print and digital collections. There are 29 bookable group study rooms, multiple spaces for groups to work together informally, and plenty of quiet and silent space.

The BJL is a place for studying and more. Meet friends for coffee in the cafeteria, take in an exhibition or catch the stunning view from the seventh floor. The open ground floor with our Art Gallery and Exhibition Hall is a welcoming place for everyone on campus and also the general public.

This announcement is a good example of the tone and style used by many libraries as they help inform their students of new learning spaces and the different types of spaces and resources available to them.

Employability

The concept of employability relates to the knowledge and understanding, skills and personal attributes which enable graduates to develop a professional career within their chosen sector. Employability is now high on the agenda of colleges and universities for a number of reasons. Increased numbers of graduates has led to greater competition for graduate jobs and following the increase in the financial costs of gaining a degree students are increasingly focused on the benefits of their investment and their future employment. Employability is one of the measures used in some of the higher education league tables and so higher education institutions are focused on improving their graduate employability record as a means of improving the reputation and success of the institution.

In addition, because of the widening participation agenda students from low-income or disadvantaged backgrounds expect their university experiences to have a positive impact on their employability. Finally, employers and employer organizations, such as the Confederation of British Industry, are keen to recruit 'work-ready' graduates who have the knowledge, skills and aptitudes necessary for working in a fast moving, digital, global environment.

In the UK, there have been a number of national initiatives and policy documents that have highlighted the importance of the graduate employability agenda for colleges and universities. Examples include:

- BIS (2011a) *Higher Education: Students at the Heart of the System.*
- Wilson (2012) *A Review of Business–University Collaboration*, which offers a critique and recommendations for developing relationships to improve student employability and employer involvement.
- BIS (2011b) *Supporting Graduate Employability.*
- Research Councils UK (2010) *Review of Progress in Implementing the Recommendations of Sir Gareth Roberts, Regarding Employability and Career Development of PhD Students and Research Staff.*

As a result of these and many other reports, colleges and universities have developed new or revised organizational employability strategies. The development of the concept of digital literacy (which encompasses information literacy) includes the idea of students developing the digital skills required for employment. A number of higher education institutions have developed graduate attributes and used them as a focus for developing a new undergraduate and postgraduate curriculum and to develop extracurricular activities. In addition, special employability awards, often involving the use of digital badges (a digital certificate), are becoming increasingly common. Following developments in digital literacy and graduate attributes, the work of library and information workers in supporting student learning is often linked to their employability and this brings new challenges and opportunities. The theme of employability is explored in more depth in Chapter 4.

Internationalization of higher education

Internationalization is high on the agenda of higher education across the world. Although, academics and students have traditionally studied, researched and collaborated with institutions in other countries, the scale of internationalization has increased immensely in the past 20 years. It is driven by a number of factors including:

- the desire of many students to study and work in different countries as a means of developing their language skills (English-speaking countries are very popular destinations), inter-cultural knowledge and experiences
- the need for many employers to recruit graduates who have the knowledge and skills required to succeed in a global community
- the increased diversification of higher education provision, e.g. transnational programmes, international partnerships, distance teaching models such as a flying faculty – one where academics and other staff fly out to teach students
- developing extensive and reliable digital environments enabling co-operative and collaborative working across traditional boundaries.

Schoorman (2000:5) provides a useful definition of internationalization:

> Internationalization is an ongoing, counter hegemonic educational process which occurs in an international context of knowledge and practice where societies are reviewed as subsystems of a larger inclusive world. The process of internationalization at an educational institution entails a comprehensive, multifaceted program of action that is integrated into every aspect of education.

The final sentence in this definition highlights the importance of higher education institutions developing appropriate strategies and practices to support internationalization. Typically, these cover areas such as:

- student mobility (incoming and outgoing)
- staff mobility (incoming and outgoing)
- different forms of educational provision: progression arrangements; collaborative degrees; study abroad (for a module, summer school, semester or whole year); exchange; and other partnership arrangements
- developing an international curriculum, which presents global perspectives, inter-cultural communications, language teaching and socially responsible citizenship
- developing international collaborative research activities (typically involving strategic partnerships).

One of the implications of the internationalization agenda is that many library and information workers are now supporting international students on campus and at a distance, and this is explored in the next chapter.

Institutional responses to change

Universities and colleges are responding to these changes in many different ways. Many are introducing major and radical change processes which involve changes to the curriculum, enhanced learning and teaching, developments of the infrastructure and new learning spaces. Examples include: Curriculum 2016 at the University of Hull (see www2.hull.ac.uk); Manchester Metropolitan University's Enhancing Quality and Assessment for Learning Programme (http://mmu.ac.uk); and Learning Futures at the University of Westminster (see case study below and www.westminster.ac.uk).

Case study: Learning Futures at the University of Westminster

The University of Westminster in London established a major change programme called Learning Futures in 2012, which was driven by the understanding that students' expectations and experiences, and learning landscapes (including the digital environment) were changing. There was a need to make a major change to prepare students for living and working in a complex and uncertain global environment.

The University reviewed its strategy and vision, and the Learning Futures programme looked at the whole learning experience – from the curriculum, assessment and regulations to the way that learning activities are designed and supported. The aim was to develop a new and very different experience for students, graduates and staff. The programme was led by the deputy vice chancellor and started with open consultation meetings and residential events, which involved students and staff from all parts of the university.

The programme developed into four key projects and is currently delivering its outcomes with a new undergraduate model due to be implemented in 2016. The projects are:

- Curriculum and Assessment: reviewed the academic framework, student assessment and regulations. It asked questions such as: How many credits in a module? How much assessment should there be and what form should it take? How can we integrate and deepen students' thinking? What is the role (if any) of synoptic assessment? The outcomes of this project resulted in a new academic framework, new regulations (co-written with students), and the extensive use of synoptic assessment.
- Transforming Learning and Teaching: reviewed learning and teaching, and technology enhanced learning. It looked at ways of making courses accessible to all. It explored different approaches to working with students (students as co-creators) and how staff could develop their approaches to learning and teaching (communities of interest and communities of practice).
- Westminster Distinctiveness: focused on employability, internationalization, including student mobility, environment and sustainability, ethics and professional practices. The

outcomes of this project resulted in developing a Westminster set of graduate attributes, digital badges, an innovative and distinct set of university-wide interdisciplinary modules, and new policies and practices to support internationalization and student mobility.

- Academic Support: this part of the project focused on developing a seamless approach to student support by providing integrated systems accessible online.

The University provided more than £2.4 million to the strategic project. It involved collaboration across the University, with team leaders selected from staff volunteers and supported by mentors and diverse teams of staff, students and the Students' Union.

In addition to the Learning Futures programme, additional associated changes are taking place at the university including:

- enhancement of student employability through an employability task force
- development of student learning spaces inside and outside the libraries
- development of the virtual learning environment
- enhancement of student record and associated systems
- introduction of a student engagement and attendance system
- enhancement of learning and teaching spaces within faculties
- research into students' digital experiences and expectations
- pedagogic research relating to Learning Futures
- development of new ways of working with 'students as co-creators'.

Library and information staff work on these changes at all levels of the institution from strategy to operational development.

Changing ways of working for library and information professionals

The changes described in the earlier sections of this chapter are all having an impact on library and information workers. Jaguszewski and Williams (2013), writing from a US perspective, provide a useful summary of some of the current trends:

- Development of user-centred library and information services which put the students, academics and researchers at the centre of the service rather than the collections.
- Development of a hybrid model of liaison librarian and functionalist specialist with liaison librarians being advocates and consultants, and working closely with specialists such as copyright and legal advisers, digital media professionals, and library and information learning and teaching.
- Introduction of organizational flexibility to meet changing user needs, which

involves different professional groups working closely together to deliver a seamless service to the users. Examples include: library liaison staff, information technologists, data managers, digital specialists and legal specialists.

- Work in new spaces with new partners. The development of new learning spaces, particularly for taught undergraduate and postgraduate students with a growing trend to develop them for research students too, means that librarians now need to work in new ways and often in partnership with other professional groups in these new shared spaces.
- Be aware of the importance of collaboration. The new and rapidly changing environment of higher education requires collaboration across traditional professional boundaries and often across higher education institutions, as well as working with new groups, such as the public.
- Create and sustain a flexible workforce. Library and information service managers nowadays need to develop a flexible workforce so that they can continue to meet the needs of their users. This requires ongoing learning and development through updating existing professional skills and developing new ones, e.g. in learning and teaching, digital media and project management.

The focus of this book is on a very specific aspect of the changing practices in library and information services: supporting student learning in higher education. The next section describes the structure of this book and provides an indication of the ways in which this theme is tackled in each of the chapters.

The structure of the book

Chapter 1 provides an insight into the current context of higher education and highlights changes that are taking place in the following areas: the learning landscape, students' experiences and expectations, the relevance of flexible learning, internationalization and student employability. It establishes the environment in which current practices in supporting student learning are changing and developing.

Chapter 2 considers the diverse nature of student populations. It starts by considering the many different forms of difference within a student population. This is followed by a discussion on students in the digital age, which complements the section on students' expectations and experiences in Chapter 1, and extends it to consider some of the implications for library and information services. Student mobility is now an important facet of academic life and the section on working with international students demonstrates their diversity. Home students have very mixed educational and library experience, too. The next section considers students with disabilities and highlights some of the forms of support for them and the kinds of typical reasonable adjustments made to support these students in their academic work. This is followed by a section on part-time students, which considers some of their distinct characteristics and their need for flexible support. The concept of learning styles is regularly critiqued but they have influenced learning and teaching practices in higher education and there is still a lively research debate about their validity. Two approaches to learning styles – multiple intelligences and the VARK system (the visual, auditory, reading or writing and kinesthetic modalities of learning) – are outlined. Chapter 2 concludes by giving tips for working with diverse groups of students.

Chapter 3 is concerned with digital literacies and covers several topics including digital literacies, information literacies including metaliteracy, and digital badges. Each section provides a definition and outline of the subject, followed by examples and case studies of current practice in libraries and information services in universities and colleges.

Chapter 4 provides an overview of different approaches to employability and explores the different ways in which library and information workers support the development of student employability. This is followed by an investigation into the many ways that students work in libraries, e.g. through work experience, academic projects and volunteering, and as co-creators; this supports their employability and helps libraries to develop and innovate.

Chapter 5 considers different approaches to learning and teaching. The models or theories explored in this chapter are Kolb's learning cycle, Laurillard's conversational framework for the effective use of learning technologies, Entwistle's teaching for understanding at university, Land and Meyer's threshold concepts, and the Higher Education Academy's work on flexible pedagogies. The different approaches to learning and teaching present a complex picture and the summary for this chapter pulls out the key ideas from each model or theory which are relevant to library and information workers' practices in supporting student learning.

Chapter 6 considers various learning activities commonly used to support student learning and which may be used by library and information workers as part of their face-to-face, blended or online courses or modules. This chapter has sections on presenting basic ideas, common learning and teaching activities, assessment of learning and reflection on learning. Activities involving the use of different technologies are considered as are more traditional methods, which require limited or no use of technology. Increasingly, library and information workers provide learning support to students using a diverse range of tools and outside of taught sessions; this topic is covered at the end of this chapter.

Chapters 7 and 8 are concerned with the design of student learning and teaching activities and events. Chapter 7 looks at the principles of course or session design, starting with a section on thinking about student learners. This is followed by a section on basic design principles including the use of aims and outcomes. Bloom's taxonomy is used to demonstrate how to identify particular levels of learning and this is associated with the idea of surface and deep learning. This is followed by sections on the design of individual learning activities, finding and using learning resources, and reviewing the programme design. The chapter concludes with a short section on marketing and promotion. Chapter 8 gives practical examples of the application of design ideas introduced in Chapter 7. It is concerned with face-to-face sessions and flipped classroom sessions, designing blended learning courses, and designing online courses.

Chapter 9 provides guidance on delivering learning experiences face to face or online. It covers the following themes: preparing yourself, face-to-face delivery, online delivery and co-facilitation. The chapter considers different stages in the delivery process: preparing for the event or course, getting off to a good start, facilitating the learning processes, and ending the event or course.

Chapter 10 is concerned with evaluation and starts with a brief overview of the UK quality control and enhancement processes, led by the Quality Assurance Agency (QAA) in the UK. These processes, or similar ones in other countries, are very relevant to library and information workers who are delivering learning and teaching activities that are part of an assessed and credit-bearing module or course. The main part of the chapter is concerned with the evaluation of the impact of learning and teaching activities and includes a summary of the research findings of Schilling and Applegate (2012), which provides an insight into the distinctions used when measuring student attitudes, learning and behaviours. This is followed by a section on practical approaches to evaluation, which covers a wide range of methods from student assignments through to tests. It includes a number of case studies that demonstrate the value of using a combination of tools when evaluating these interventions.

The final chapter explores different approaches to keeping up to date and developing one's professional profile. This is particularly important given the rapidly changing environment and the increased emphasis on online networking as a form of professional development. This chapter considers the following topics: networking through professional organizations; learning in the workplace; accredited courses; short courses, conferences and workshops; independent learning; developing online networks; and managing the short term immediate needs and longer term career planning of individual professional development.

Summary
This chapter has introduced the reader to current themes and issues in higher education and explained that these are changing many practices within colleges and universities. The landscape of learning and teaching is changing. This is illustrated by changes to the learning environment within and outside libraries, and by changes to the digital landscape, which is developing at an extremely rapid pace. Our student body has become extremely diverse, and students are coming to university with very diverse digital experiences and high expectations about

the digital environment and the digital skills of academic and support staff. Employability is high on the agenda for students and higher education institutions, and one response has been to integrate it into the curriculum and to enhance extracurricular activities on this subject. Others are to look at ideas about learning and teaching, and recognize the need for more flexibility – learning where the learner can control the pace, place and/or mode of their study. These changes have implications for all library and information workers in higher education.

References

Beetham, H. and White, D. (2013) *Students' Expectations and Experiences of the Digital Environment*, Facet Publishing.

BIS (2011a) *Higher Education: Students at the Heart of the System*, Department for Business Innovation and Skills, https://www.gov.uk/government/uploads/system/uploads/attachment_data/file/31384/11-944-higher-education-students-at-heart-of-system.pdf.

Department for Business Innovation and Skills (2011b) *Supporting Graduate Employability: HEI practice in other countries*, https://www.gov.uk/government/uploads/system/uploads/attachment_data/file/32421/11-913-supporting-graduate-employability-other-countries.pdf.

Freed, B. (2015) State-of-the-art Medical Library Opens Without Books, *Designing Libraries*, http://designinglibraries.org.uk/index.asp?PageID=609.

Gordon, N. (2014) *Flexible Pedagogies: technology-enhanced learning*, Higher Education Academy.

Jaguszewski, J. and Williams, K. (2013) New Roles for New Times: transforming liaison roles in research libraries, http://conservancy.umn.edu/handle/11299/169867.

Leadership Foundation for Higher Education (2014) *Changing the Learning Landscape: final report 2012–2014*, www.lfhe.ac.uk/en/programmes-events/your-university/cll/.

McLinden, M. (2013) *Flexible Pedagogies: part time learning and learners, Final Report*, Higher Education Academy.

Research Councils UK (2010) *Review of Progress in Implementing the Recommendations of Sir Gareth Roberts, Regarding Employability and Career Development of PhD Students and Research Staff: a report for Research Councils UK by an independent review panel*, www.rcuk.ac.uk/RCUK-prod/assets/documents/skills/IndependentReviewHodge.pdf.

Schilling, K. and Applegate, R. (2012) Best Methods for Evaluating Educational Impact: a comparison of the efficacy of commonly used measures of library instruction, *Journal of the Medical Library Association: JMLA*, **100** (4), 258.

Schoorman, D. (2000) What Do We Mean by Internationalization?, *Contemporary Education*, **71** (4), 5–7.

Wilson, H. (2015) Libraries Without Walls: when students become the core design consideration, www.architectureanddesign.com.au/features/comment/libraries-without-walls-when-students-become-the-c.

Wilson, T. (2012) *A Review of Business–University Collaboration*, https://www.gov.uk/government/uploads/system/uploads/attachment_data/file/32383/12-610-wilson-review-business-university-collaboration.pdf.

2

Working with students

Introduction

This chapter provides an overview of students in colleges and universities, and different ways of working with them. Student populations in higher education are extremely diverse and the following themes and categories are explored in this chapter: students in the digital age; international students; students with disabilities; part-time students; and diversity as a result of individual learning styles. This is followed by a section on the implications of diverse student populations on learning and teaching.

Diverse student populations

Over the last 20 years there has been an explosion in university enrolments in most countries across the world (UNESCO, 2015). In the UK many colleges and universities highlight their diverse student populations in their marketing materials, often stating that their students come from more than 100 or even 150 countries. This gives students advantages through studying with others from different countries and creating lifetime global networks.

The diversity of student populations goes well beyond students' home backgrounds. These are some of the different factors related to diverse student populations that affect a student's experience:

- academic skills
- age
- cultural background
- digital skills
- educational experiences
- emotional intelligence
- emotional resilience
- employment experiences
- ethnic background

- faith
- financial situation
- gender
- health
- information technology skills
- language
- learning styles
- life experiences
- literacy and numeracy
- mental health
- nationality
- previous educational experiences
- special needs.

Students who appear superficially to come from the same background may be very different, as illustrated in the following example.

Example: Two students from Guangzhou, China

This example is based on the author's experience of teaching Chinese students in a UK university in the north of England. As part of an induction activity, the students were asked to introduce themselves to the whole class. Names have been changed to protect their identity.

One student, Amy Ho, explained that she had attended a British boarding school in Yorkshire for five years and had obtained four A levels and 12 GCSEs. Her family lived in Guangzhou and she was used to travelling from the UK to Guangzhou for her holidays, though she often holidayed in Dubai and Australia.

In contrast, Zheng Zhu had attended a school in Guangzhou and then had completed a foundation year in a private sector Chinese college which had partnered with the university. On successful completion of the foundation year he had transferred to the UK northern university. He had never been outside China before travelling to the UK to enrol as a student.

When supporting student learning, the implications of working with very diverse groups of students is that care needs to be taken during the planning and delivery of all kinds of courses and programmes (face to face, blended learning, online learning) so that all the students are able to achieve the learning outcomes and feel comfortable in the learning environment.

Students in the digital age

Chapter 1 briefly introduced the changing learning landscape, including the student experience and expectations. This section considers students in the digital age in more depth. Research and popular literature indicates that there has been much interest in the implications of the digital age and widespread access to many technologies for students. Labels such as 'digital natives' – students who have grown up surrounded by different technologies, multimedia and the internet – and 'digital immigrants' – students who were not born into the digital world but have adopted these technologies at some point in their lives (Prensky, 2001) – are used. It is now widely recognized that students are extremely diverse in their uses and adoption of technology and this is not necessarily a generational characteristic. This is clearly articulated by Jones and Shao (2011, 2): 'The evidence indicates that young students do not form a generational cohort and they do not express consistent or generationally organized demands.'

Jones and Shao (2011) report that there is little evidence to suggest that there is a single new generation of students entering higher education with a homogenous approach to their use of different technologies. However, a number of factors, including age, gender, mode of study (distance learning or campus based) and their international or home status, have an impact on students' use of digital media. In addition, there is huge variety among academic staff in their use of new technology in support of student learning in the classroom, on campus or at a distance. Complex changes are taking place, which include the use of social networking sites such as Facebook, multimedia through sites such as YouTube, and mobile devices including apps. Jones and Shao (2011, 2) suggest that:

> Universities should be confident in the provision of what might seem to be basic services. Students appreciate and make use of the foundational infrastructure for learning, even where this is often criticized as being an out of date and unimaginative use of new technology. Virtual learning environments (learning or course management systems) are used widely and seem to be well regarded. The provision by university libraries of online services, including the provision of online e-journals and e-books, are also positively received.

They advise that where different technologies are used within a course they should be used for sound pedagogic reasons and be well planned and implemented within the curriculum.

Beetham (2014), writing a Jisc blog on students' experiences and expectations of the digital environment, identified that students expect the following from their universities or colleges: ubiquitous wifi; the ability to connect their own devices to university systems easily; and continued access to university technologies, particularly desktop computers with access to relevant software. She writes: 'Students need a flexible environment that lets them experiment, learn from each other, and create their own blend.'

Case study: Student voices

Jisc (2014) has produced a series of posters which highlight the student voice with headlines such as:

I need high-speed broadband for my digital services – everywhere, and all the time.

I want to be able to use my own device(s) on campus.

Let me use my own search engines to find my own content.

Lecturers should be able to manage the data projector without embarrassing themselves.

I expect the technology I use here to be better than the technology I have at home or in school.

Please don't make IT induction compulsory – everyone knows that stuff these days.

I want my course to equip me for the job market, and that means digital skills.

I expect other students to be up to speed with online systems, otherwise they'll hold me back when we're doing group work.

The findings from Beetham's research show that students need to be involved in two-way discussions so that they learn how different technologies may have a transformative effect on their approach to studying and future careers. In addition, she emphasizes the importance of working with students as partners, co-creating learning spaces and developing the university's digital environment. Beetham (2014) reports that students are concerned about the need to develop their presence and online identity, and that this is something they may develop within the security of the university.

Working with international students

The concept of internationalization was introduced in Chapter 1. One aspect of internationalization is student mobility, an important feature of contemporary higher education, particularly in the many English-speaking countries or English-speaking colleges or universities that are important destinations for international students. For example, undergraduate and postgraduate courses in the UK are likely to attract relatively large numbers of international students; in some instances international students comprise as much as 95–100% of all students on a course.

There is an ever-growing literature on this subject and some of it presents over-simplistic views of these students and their learning experiences both before they come to the UK and afterwards. Montgomery (2010) has produced a detailed study of international students and their experiences within the UK. Her work is particularly interesting as, in addition to a literature review, she provides insights into the daily lives of seven international students from countries such as China, India, Nepal, Indonesia, Italy and the Netherlands over six months. Montgomery's work challenges stereotypes about international students who may be labelled as slow learners with poor English, who have never had the opportunity to move beyond rote learning and have no experience of group work or speaking up in class. According to Montgomery, a common stereotype that some academics believe is that these students are much more likely to cheat, e.g. through poor or no referencing skills, and not understand or want to understand the importance of academic integrity or ethical behaviour.

In contrast to the stereotype, her findings illustrate that the students involved in her study are highly motivated, mature, keen to learn, very focused on their studies and aware of the benefits of higher education. They do experience an initial adjustment period and once this is over they are likely to achieve more than local students. These students are studying in an English-speaking country as they wish to develop their language skills as English is the global language for business and industry. They are proud of their own culture and languages, and want to develop themselves as global players in their chosen career.

The English language skills of international students vary considerably. Some speak and write English impeccably. Others need to adapt to the accents and rhythms experienced in everyday academic life, but once they adjust to local or regional accents they have no difficulty in using the English language. In contrast, some students struggle with English and so find their taught sessions a challenge. Colleges and universities offer additional academic English courses to help support these students.

International students come from very varied educational institutions, including prestigious research institutions, colleges and universities that are focused on learning and teaching, and private education providers. It is a very complex picture so it is important to learn as much as possible about partner institutions within your country or overseas.

Educational practices vary from country to country and within countries, culture to culture, and institution to institution. These are some areas of difference:

- The connections between learning, teaching and research may be weak or strong.
- The focus in the classroom can vary from being teacher focused to being student focused or a combination of both (see Chapter 5).
- The role of the textbook can vary: it might be the only information source used in a course or be one of many sources, or there may be no textbooks.
- The types and forms of assessment vary, from a total exam regime to one of assignments and/or portfolios.
- Access to information technologies may vary from there being 100% access through to limited or no access to online resources.

- Opportunities for academic writing (beyond examination answers) can be very different, and styles of writing can range from the extremely formal, e.g. use of the third person, to informal styles of writing.
- Use of referencing by students and staff can differ hugely.
- Access to libraries and other forms of support may be very varied. For example: some students have had access to world-class university libraries and resources; in some countries postgraduate students have full access to the university libraries while undergraduate students have no or little access; students studying in private sector educational institutions may have very limited access to a library and/or access to online resources.

Although this section is concerned with international students, the list of different educational practices applies equally to home students, who are likely to have had very varied prior educational experiences, coming from public and private sector schools and colleges, distance learning colleges, further education colleges, private providers and other universities.

Frequently, the first contact that library and information workers have with international students is at induction and orientation events. This is also the time that those students who have recently arrived in the country are experiencing culture shock and having to adapt to possibly different approaches to learning and teaching. Therefore it is not a good time to inform these students about the intricacies of libraries, database searching, referencing or plagiarism. It is sensible to restrict induction or orientation sessions to presenting a few key points and signposting the students to future events.

There are many resources on working with international students. Colleges and universities often have an international office whose staff may provide helpful advice and guidance via short courses, guidance materials and their websites. Many organizations that provide support for international students have helpful websites, e.g. the UK Council for International Student Affairs (see www.ukcisa.org.uk), as do some publishers, e.g. Palgrave (www.palgrave.com/skills4study/).

Students with disabilities

In many countries disabled students have rights to protect them from discrimination. The United Nations Convention on Disability Rights helps to enforce, protect and promote these rights. In the UK, the Equality Act 2010 identifies these rights, which cover areas such as employment, and colleges and universities have a duty to make reasonable adjustments so that all disabled students (not just UK citizens) are not placed at a substantial disadvantage in their learning.

The Equality Act defines a disabled person as someone who has a physical or mental impairment that has a substantial and long-term adverse effect on his or her ability to carry out normal day-to-day activities. This may include:

- a specific learning difficulty
- a visual impairment
- a hearing impairment
- a mobility impairment
- a mental health condition
- other unseen conditions.

Specialist support services within colleges and universities provide advice and support to students and staff. Learning and teaching support is likely to include:

- assessment of needs (or referral to an assessment centre)
- reasonable adjustment within learning and teaching sessions:
  — access to all learning materials in advance of the session
  — permission to record sessions (audio and/or video)
  — one-to-one support, e.g. note takers
  — advice on using enabling technologies
- reasonable adjustments relating to assessment:
  — additional writing time
  — rest breaks
  — use of an amanuensis (scribe)
  — use of a reader
  — use of assistive technology, specialist software or a PC
  — an alternative exam room
  — a separate room within the department
  — use of coloured overlays in exams
  — examination papers in alternative formats, e.g. large print or Braille
  — use of specialist equipment, e.g. chair or writing slope
  — use of specialist software
  — timetabling of exams in morning or afternoon sessions only
  — alternative assessment, e.g. an assignment instead of an examination
- support for independent study:
  — provision of learning materials in alternative formats
  — loans of specialist equipment
  — one-to-one support
  — specialist workshops.

Library and information services often have a member of staff who is designated to co-ordinate support for students with disabilities and libraries are often used as a means of offering assistive technologies and equipment (e.g. accessible furniture, assistive technologies and software, and auxiliary aids) and special services such as workshops, individual induction and tours, help with using assistive technologies, access to materials in alternative formats, and help with finding specific items. These are normally advertised on the library website and students with disabilities are encouraged to speak to a librarian so that the appropriate support can be put in place.

The library disability co-ordinator may work closely with a faculty or department-based academic disability tutor, whose role is to support students with a disability. They act as a link between the disability services unit and students with disabilities, and use their specialist knowledge of learning and teaching within their subject area and knowledge in the field of disability.

Individual universities and colleges provide information and advice, and train staff to support students with disabilities. Frequently this information is given online (e.g. through the open website or the virtual learning environment) by specialist disability support staff.

Part-time students

HEFCE's report *Pressure from all Sides* (2014) identifies the pressures on part-time students and highlights the rapid decline in part-time UK and European Union student numbers. The report relates this to a number of factors, such as the cost of studying for a degree; the economic climate, which has resulted in a decline in the numbers of employers willing to support staff development; reduced employment opportunities, particularly in the public sector; increased financial pressures on individuals and their families; and the impact of student debt on an individual's decision to progress to postgraduate study. Although many of these factors are also relevant to full-time students, the characteristics of part-time students means that the impact is greater on their access to higher education.

Pollard, Newton and Hillage (2012) state that part-time students have characteristics that are distinct from full-time students. They:

- are older and more likely to be female
- are more likely to come from a widening participation (under-represented) background if they are young
- are often concentrated in large cities or in deprived and coastal areas
- are more likely than full-time students to come from areas where it is uncommon for people to go into higher education
- often have caring or other family responsibilities.

Pollard, Newton and Hillage's work considers the study profiles of part-time students, which are distinct from full timers. They are likely to:

- enroll on short professional development courses
- enroll on programmes of study which last more than four years

- study on courses equivalent to two-thirds of a full-time-equivalent course
- study subjects allied to health (mostly nursing and social work), education, business and administrative studies, and social studies.

Part-time students may attend classes during the day or evening and work in cohorts with full-time students, or attend courses which have been established for part-time-only students. Many universities' systems and processes are determined by the needs of full-time undergraduate students, with notable exceptions such as the Open University. They may therefore not be sufficiently flexible in supporting the needs of part-time students, who may only be on site for relatively short periods of time and are pressured by their work and other commitments. For example, study support and information literacy workshops may only be scheduled on a weekday rather than during the evening or at the weekend when part-time students may be more likely to be able to take part in them. The shift to 24/7 library access with an increasing number of online tutorials and support systems is particularly helpful for many part-time students.

Diverse learning styles

The concept of 'learning styles' is based on the idea that individuals have different learning preferences. It originated in the 1970s and there is now a huge number of different models and theories of learning styles, and an extensive research literature built around testing the validity of different models (and their associated tools) and critiquing the concept. See for example, Pashler et al. (2008); Sanderson (2011); Vasquez (2009); Willingham, Hughes and Dobolyi (2015). These models and theories still influence learning and teaching within colleges and universities, including library and information settings, and the idea of learning styles continues to influence theories and models of information literacy. For example, the concept of multiple intelligences (outlined below) influenced the development of ideas about metaliteracy (Mackey and Jacobson, 2014), which is explored in Chapter 3.

Example: Personal practice

In my practice of working with students, I use models of learning styles, e.g. Honey and Mumford (1994) and the concept of multiple intelligences (developed by Howard Gardner (1993, 2011) as a means of engaging students to reflect on their approaches to learning. I find that they provide a useful framework for thinking and talking about learning and teaching. Sometimes I use them in induction and orientation sessions as a means of helping students to think about their approaches to learning in a structured way. They also help to demonstrate the diversity of students in their approaches to learning and teaching. However, I always emphasize that these models should not be used to label oneself, and individuals are so sophisticated that our approaches to learning and teaching change over time and context.

Multiple intelligences

Howard Gardner (1993, 2011) developed the concept of multiple intelligences, the idea that eight abilities make up intelligence: linguistic ability, logical–mathematical ability, musical ability, bodily kinesthetic ability, spatial–visual ability, interpersonal ability, intrapersonal ability and naturalistic ability. An additional two abilities have since been added by Gardner to his original eight: spiritual or existential ability, and moral ability. It is worth noting that Gardner's approach was to use this knowledge to empower learners rather than to label them with a specific intelligence. An extensive range of online and paper-based tests are available for use in teaching and learning situations.

Example: Use of Gardner's concept of multiple intelligences in a large class lecture

I have used Gardner's multiple intelligences concept in a lecture within a first-year undergraduate module on academic skills. The aim of the lecture was to introduce the concept of reflection on learning. Using a range of media, I presented each of the original eight multiple intelligences on a PowerPoint slide.

I asked the students to consider their responses to each of the multiple intelligences in the context of a subject they enjoyed, and one they found challenging, giving them five minutes to do so. I then asked them to discuss their reflections with their neighbour(s) and to consider the implications, if any, for them as new undergraduate students. I emphasized that this was an exercise in reflection and that they were not to use their findings to label themselves; they were not being asked to use a valid and reliable scientific tool. I suggested that their findings provided a snapshot in time on how they thought about their approaches to learning and these were likely to change as they engaged with their degree. The students enjoyed the activity and engaged with it, and it gave them the opportunity to talk to their neighbours (an important part of the socialization process during the first few weeks of the semester).

The lecture and activity were linked to a formative assessment task, which required students to evaluate the concept of learning styles using a selection of peer-reviewed articles in academic journals and also articles in professional journals. The formative assessment task was followed up in a seminar and led into students working on their summative assessment task for the module.

VARK system

The VARK approach to learning styles is much simpler than the concept of multiple intelligences as it is based on the idea of four modalities of learning – visual, auditory, reading or writing and kinesthetic – developed by Fleming and Mills (1992). According to this model, visual learners prefer to learn via diagrams, images, illustrations and pictures; auditory learners learn best by listening, e.g. to lectures, recordings or discussions; people with a preference for reading or writing learn best through methods; and kinesthetic or tactile learners prefer to learn practical experiences including hands-on work.

Case study: Developing online tutorials using the VARK system

Walters et al. (2015) describe the development of online tutorials designed to improve the information literacy of second-year nursing students. Their development process involved focusing on three main areas: information behaviour, learning technologies and the VARK system. The latter was used to inform the team about learning styles so that they could match the course delivery to the full range of styles.

Practical approaches for working with diverse groups of students

This chapter explores the individual learning styles of diverse student groups. In this section, I draw together these ideas to provide a set of tips, which are applicable to working with all student groups.

When preparing your session:

- Provide learning materials including presentations in advance.
- Provide a glossary of terms.
- Use a variety of learning and teaching activities.
- Use visual and auditory methods.
- Include practical work with feedback.
- Provide examples of 'good work'.
- Use international examples.
- Avoid stereotypes in examples and case studies.
- Use examples that are inclusive.
- Ensure that images are representative of wider society.
- Consider recording your sessions so that students can listen to or view them again (this is becoming normal practice in many higher education institutions).

During your session:

- Provide clear guidance throughout the session, e.g. 'We are going to do three activities, the first one is . . .'
- Let students know your expectations, e.g. whether they should ask questions during or after any presentation.
- Avoid culture-specific idioms, proverbs and analogies.
- Keep your language neutral.
- Avoid rhetorical questions as they can cause confusion.
- Think carefully before using humour.
- Use pair and small group work to help everyone engage with the course.
- Give students advance warning that they may be asked to speak. This gives them time to prepare their thoughts.
- Ask individuals who are quiet for their opinions and thoughts.

- Cater for non-native speakers and students with high level language ability.
- Accept native tongue discussions.
- Let students know that you have an interest in their culture and background.
- Draw on students' past experiences.
- Use short quizzes to encourage student interactions.
- Make sure everyone can hear and understand contributions from all students.
- Challenge discriminatory language or behaviours.
- Think about what you say and do, and its impact on the whole group.
- If you are concerned that you are not making reasonable adjustments to meet the needs of individuals find out more about how you can provide the necessary support.

After your session:

- Follow up any outstanding queries or comments.
- If required, provide additional learning resources.
- Reflect on your session and how it could be improved in future.

Summary

The main message from this chapter is that students in higher education are extremely diverse. Specific areas covered include: students in the digital age, the diversity of students, international students, students with disabilities, and part-time students. The implications for supporting the learning of diverse groups of students is summarized in a series of tips which highlight important points to take into account when preparing your session, during the learning and teaching session, and afterwards.

References

Beetham, H. (2014) *Students' Experiences and Expectations of the Digital Environment*, https://www.jisc.ac.uk/blog/students-experiences-and-expectations-of-the-digital-environment-23-jun-2014/.

Fleming, N. D. and Mills, C. E. (1992) Not Another Inventory, Rather a Catalyst for Reflection, *To Improve the Academy*, **11**, 137.

Gardner, H. (1993) *Multiple Intelligences: the theory in practice*, Basic Books.

Gardner, H. (2011) *Frames of Mind: the theory of multiple intelligences*, Basic Books.

HEFCE (2014) *Pressure From All Sides: economic and policy influences on part-time higher education*, www.hefce.ac.uk/pubs/year/2014/201408d/.

Honey, P. and Mumford, A. (1994) *Manual of Learning Styles*, Peter Honey Publishing.

Jisc (2014) *Digital Students are Different*, poster set, bit.ly/jisc-digitalstudentproject.

Jones, C. and Shao, B. (2011) *The Net Generation and Digital Natives: implications for higher education*, Higher Education Academy.

Mackey, T. P. and Jacobson, T. E. (2014) *Metaliteracy: reinventing information literacy to empower learners*, Facet Publishing.

Montgomery, C. (2010) *Understanding the International Student Experience*, Palgrave Macmillan.

Pashler, H., McDaniel, M., Rohrer, D. and Bjork, R. (2008) Learning Styles Concepts and Evidence, *Psychological Science in the Public Interest*, **9** (3), 105–19.

Pollard, E., Newton, B. and Hillage, J. (2012) *Expanding and Improving Part-time Higher Education*, BIS Research Paper 68, 277, https://www.gov.uk/government/uploads/system/uploads/attachment_data/file/32397/12-906-expanding-improving-part-time-higher-education.pdf.

Prensky, M. (2001) Digital Natives, Digital Immigrants, *On the Horizon*, **9** (5), 1–6.

Sanderson, H. (2011) Using Learning Styles in Information Literacy: critical considerations for librarians, *The Journal of Academic Librarianship*, **37** (5), 376–85.

UNESCO (2015) *Higher Education Statistics*, www.uis.unesco.org/.

Vasquez, K. (2009) Learning Styles as Self-fulfilling Prophecies. In Gurung, R. A. R. and Prieto, L. R. *Getting Culture: incorporating diversity across the curriculum*, Stylus, 53–63.

Walters, K., Bolich, C., Duffy, D., Quinn, C., Walsh, K. and Connolly, S. (2015) Developing Online Tutorials to Improve Information Literacy Skills for Second-year Nursing Students of University College Dublin, *New Review of Academic Librarianship*, **21** (1), 7–29.

Willingham, D. T., Hughes, E. M. and Dobolyi, D. G. (2015) The Scientific Status of Learning Styles Theories, *Teaching of Psychology*, **42** (3), 266–71.

3

Digital literacies

Introduction

Employability is high on the agenda for colleges and universities, and there is a recognition that students and graduates need a wide range of professional skills, including digital and information skills, in order to be successful on their degree course and as they enter the wider world of work.

Traditionally, the library and information profession has always 'owned' information literacy, but recently a broader concept of digital literacies has developed. This has resulted in new ways of thinking and working within higher education as different professional groups, e.g. library and information workers, media support workers, IT trainers and careers professionals, all have a stake in this important area. At the same time, library and information workers are engaging in areas which were traditionally outside their remit, such as student employability.

In recent years, there has been much research and many practical developments on supporting student learning in the digital age. This is explored in this chapter by looking at digital literacies, information literacies including metaliteracy, and digital badges. Chapter 4 explores the concept of employability and responses of contemporary academic libraries to students' employability.

Digital literacies in practice

Rapid changes in technology such as the rise in social media and the development of accessible media have an impact on learning and teaching, and graduate employability in universities. At one time, the institutional virtual learning environment and e-mails were the main communication channels in the learning and teaching process, and academic administration. Nowadays, there is a much more complex situation as staff and students in colleges and universities use many different systems and technologies to do their work, such as e-mail, text messages, Twitter, LinkedIn, YouTube, Flickr, SlideShare, Pressi, Pinterest, Facebook, WhatsApp, Instagram and Tumblr, as well as the institutional virtual learning environment.

Josefsson et al. (2015) have carried out research into students' use of social media and they identify three roles: the educational role, the professional role and the private role. They consider the differences between social media usage by students, and suggest that colleges and universities have a clear role in educating students to use social media as part of their studies and in preparation for work. Graduates also use many different systems in their work, and employers expect them to be able to use them to a professional level.

Jisc (2014) defines digital literacies as the capabilities which fit someone for living, learning and working in a digital society, and lists seven elements of digital literacies:

- information literacy: the ability to identify, interpret, evaluate, manage and share information
- media literacy: the ability to critically read and creatively produce academic and professional communications in a range of media
- communications and collaboration: the ability to participate in digital networks for learning and research
- digital scholarship: the ability to participate in emerging academic, professional and research practices that depend on digital systems
- ICT literacy: the ability to adopt, adapt and use digital devices, applications and services
- learning skills: the ability to study and learn effectively in technology-rich environments, formal and informal
- career and identity management: the ability to manage digital reputation and online identity.

There is now an extensive range of research and resources relating to digital literacy. For example, Jisc has invested its resources into exploring digital literacy; an example of its work may be found at https://www.jisc.ac.uk/guides/developing-students-digital-literacy. The following case studies provide examples of current practices, illustrating:

- a learning resource – an open access online quiz on digital literacy
- an event designed to support students' development in digital literacy
- an organizational action involving the development of a framework, guidance for students and staff, plus access to online learning resources.

Case study: Reflecting on digital literacy

The University of Exeter provides an open access online quiz, which enables students to identify and reflect on their digital literacy. The quiz involves answering 30 questions and the results are clearly presented under catchy headings such as:

- digital dodger
- digital guru
- information junkie
- career builder
- media mogul
- online networker.

This quiz could be used by students in preparation for a teaching session or workshop on digital literacies.

See http://as.exeter.ac.uk/support/staffdevelopment/aspectsofacademicpractice/ assessmentandfeedback/work-integratedassessmentthecollaborateproject/the_itest__how_ digitally_literate_are_you_/.

Case study: Get the Digital Edge

At the University of Westminster, a number of professional support staff (including librarians, careers staff and technologists) work together with the Students' Union to present a series of events, one at each of its London sites, called Get the Digital Edge. The events are designed to help students to make the most of their online profile persona in preparation for the workplace by:

- learning how easily employers can find out about them online
- discovering the dos and don'ts of social media
- creating a winning LinkedIn profile
- sharing their favourite app.

Figure 3.1 shows a typical programme.

A programme of events focusing on social media, digital skills and employability. Learn how to hone your skills to get the digital edge.
12.00: Welcome
12.05: App swap. Find out from other delegates their favourite app and share your own.
12.30: Manage your online reputation. Careers advisors talk about why it is so important for your future career to manage your online identity and how you can make improvements.
13.00: Dos and don'ts of social media. A librarian shares top tips on using social media effectively.
13.30: Using library sources for job search and sector information. Library staff show you how to use company databases to research prospective employers before that all important interview.
14.00: LinkedIn workshop. Students Union Vice President provides his expertise on creating a winning LinkedIn profile.
14.30: Close

Figure 3.1 *The programme of Get the Digital Edge*

In addition to the programme Get the Digital Edge is an extensive range of online resources, including videos, which students (and staff) may access at any time.

Case study: The Open University's digital literacy framework

The Open University presents its digital literacy framework at www.open.ac.uk/libraryservices/ beingdigital/. The framework includes a definition of digital literacy, which clearly outlines the difference between digital and information literacy: 'Digital literacy includes the ability to find and use information (otherwise known as information literacy) but goes beyond this to encompass communication, collaboration and teamwork, social awareness in the digital environment, understanding of e-safety and creation of new information. Both digital and information literacy are underpinned by critical thinking and evaluation.'

The Open University also presents a general library services framework (at www.open.ac.uk/libraryservices), which gives a common reference point for staff in developing modules and courses, and helps to ensure that digital literacy is integrated into the student learning experience. The framework is divided into five competence areas, which can be viewed individually:

- being able to understand and engage in digital practices
- being able to find information
- being able to evaluate information, online interactions and online tools critically
- being able to manage and communicate information
- being able to collaborate and share digital content.

The framework describes the five stages of development of digital literacy skills, which are mapped against the different levels of academic study:

- access (Level 0)
- foundation digital practice stage (Level 1)
- interactive and co-operative digital practice stage (Level 2)
- personalized and collaborative digital practice stage (Level 3)
- professional and digital identity stage (master's degree).

The Open University has mapped each competency against different stages as shown in the following example for the competency: Critically evaluate information and online interactions and online tools:

- Distinguish between examples of information of high and low quality on the web (Level 0).
- Identify and apply appropriate quality criteria to evaluate pre-defined information, including personal contacts (Level 1).
- Apply appropriate quality criteria to evaluate a range of resources (Level 2).

- Use appropriate quality criteria to critically evaluate information from any source to determine authority, bias etc (Level 3).
- Engage in critical appraisal, including judgements on reliability and validity, of own work and the work of others (master's level).

Various support materials are associated with the framework. The Being Digital site (www.open.ac.uk/libraryservices/beingdigital/) contains many bite-size learning materials (each taking no more than ten minutes to complete) and a self-assessment checklist. These are accessible via any mobile device or desktop computer. The site also provides access to information about live events. These are examples of topics covered:

- how to present yourself to best advantage online and manage your digital identity
- how to make the most of online networks
- how to know who and what to trust online
- how to use Wikipedia
- how to evaluate and use online tools
- how to search effectively.

Finally, the site has information about accessibility, using statements such as:

- 'Activities can be accessed using keystrokes.'
- 'Accessible PDFs are available for all activities.'
- 'Text can be read using a screen reader such as JAWS. Some interactive elements such as drag and drop cannot be read with JAWS. You are advised to use the accessible PDF in these cases.'
- 'Some activities on the site feature third party material. Where this is not fully accessible a transcript or alternative version has been provided.'

Not surprisingly, this framework and the associated resources has won a number of awards. It is well worth visiting and exploring this website: www.open.ac.uk/libraryservices/pages/dilframework/.

Information literacy

The term 'information literacy' is attributed to Zurkowski (1974) and has been defined in many different ways by library professional bodies and government agencies. A broad and ambitious definition comes from UNESCO (2005): 'Information literacy empowers people in all walks of life to seek, evaluate, use and create information effectively to achieve their personal, social, occupational and educational goals. It is a basic human right in a digital world and promotes social inclusion in all nations.'

There is an extensive literature on information literacy. Secker and Coonan (2013) outline the different ways in which the term is used and its overlap (indicted with *italics*) with other concepts as follows:

- information literacy, critical thinking and evaluation, *study skills and academic writing, transliteracies, search skills, critical analysis*
- academic literacies, learning development, *study skills and academic writing*
- new literacies, multimodal learning, *transliteracies*
- digital literacy, ethics and e-safety, computer literacy and functional skills, *search skills*
- media literacy, critical use of non-textual communication formats, *critical analysis*.

Rapid changes in technology, e.g. the development of Web 2.0 and global networking, and new ideas about learning and teaching, such as flexible pedagogies and threshold concepts, have resulted in a shift in thinking about information literacy. In essence, there appears to be a change from a reductive, linear, skills-based approach to one that recognizes the messy, reflective, content and context-based practice of information literacy (Kutner and Armstrong, 2012).

The emergence of new theoretical models and theories of information literacy provides potentially valuable frameworks for informing information literacy learning and teaching. This shift is demonstrated through the recent development of new information literacy models; four models, out of the many current models, have been selected as they are having a major influence on the ways in which library and information workers are now thinking about supporting student learners. They are:

- *Framework for Information Literacy for Higher Education* (ACRL, 2014)
- *InfoFlow (Information Flow) An Integrated Model of Applied Information Literacy* (McNicol, 2014)
- *A New Curriculum for Information Literacy* (Secker and Coonan, 2013)
- *Metaliteracy* (Mackey and Jacobson, 2014).

Framework for Information Literacy for Higher Education

The *Framework for Information Literacy for Higher Education* was published by the ACRL (2014) and is based around six threshold concepts (see Chapter 5 for a discussion of threshold concepts). It is very different from the previous ACRL standards, which outlined competencies, skills and outcomes that a student needed to achieve in order to become information literate. The six frames are:

- scholarship is a conversation
- research as inquiry
- authority is contextual and constructed
- format as process

- searching as exploration
- information has value.

This framework is well worth exploring as it demonstrates a move away from the traditional linear approach to teaching information literacy to an approach which acknowledges the complex and ever changing nature of knowledge. It is worth noting that ACRL has not retired its current standards; they may be used alongside the new framework.

There is a rapidly developing literature and media base on the new framework and its implications for library and information staff; the ACRL website (see www.ala.org/acrl) is a useful starting point. A helpful publication on this subject is *Teaching Information Literacy Threshold Concepts* by Bravender, McClure and Schaub (eds) (2015).

Case study: Redeveloping a course with the new ACRL framework

Carncross (2015) provides a critical analysis of her approach to re-designing an elective module designed to help students develop their academic research skills. The previous version of the module was tightly linked to the 'old' ACRL standards. She writes:

> *My biggest issue with the standards was how tidy IL [information literacy] seemed under its prescription. The document describes a universe where one can 'determine the extent of an information need', where search strategies are 'designed', and useful information is 'extracted'. My students' actual information seeking-process involved a lot more uncertainty, a lot more trial and error.*
>
> (Carncross, 2015, 248–9)

Carncross's first step was to review the old learning objectives and re-write them (if required) to meet the new framework. She presents a table summarizing her work and the following example illustrates the difference between the old standards and the new framework approaches.

The old learning objective:

- critically evaluate information using sets of self-defined criteria (old objective – informed by standards)

was replaced by two re-written learning objectives:

- understand the concept of authority as it relates to research (new objective – informed by framework)
- critically evaluate information using sets of self-defined, question-specific criteria (new objective – informed by framework).

Following the revision of the learning objectives to meet the new framework, Carncross (2015, 250) re-visited her class tests and the summative assessment activities for the course so that they were aligned to the new objectives. This did not necessarily make it necessary to start from scratch as she used many of the sample assignments included in the framework as her starting point. One activity involved students observing and analysing scholarly conversations taking place through social media. Apparently students found it challenging to identify experts in a field and locate their online presence. This work was designed to help students to understand that authority is not necessarily hierarchical and that researchers do engage with others outside the silos of peer-reviewed academic journals. As a result of the inclusion of the concept of 'metacognition' and 'metaliteracy' in the framework, she introduced the requirement for students to keep a learning journal, which would enable them to reflect on their developing abilities. One interesting observation in her paper is that her students developed 'stronger, more intriguing research questions'.

Carncross (2015) lists some of the challenges and benefits involved in implementing the new ACRL framework. She concludes that the conceptually based framework is more closely aligned to professional thinking and developments than the old standards. However, she considers that it is hard to translate the broad concepts into learning objectives and assessment activities. The real benefit of using the new framework was that it gave an impetus for deeper reflection and greater internalization of the concepts found in the framework, and that it required additional research as well as trial and error. In other words, it provides an impetus for professional growth and development, and a renewal of information literacy learning and teaching.

InfoFlow

InfoFlow (Information Flow) is based on learning activities developed at Aalto University, Finland and it is an integrated model of applied information literacy. Detailed information about the model is available from McNicol (2014) and McNicol and Shields (2014) provide a critical review of the model and its development. The model is made up of eight elements:

- ask
- show
- make
- reflect
- map
- imagine
- explore
- collaborate.

InfoFlow is designed to support student engagement and student-centred learning; it involves a number of elements (listed above), which may be undertaken in any order. Some elements may be repeated while others may not be used during a particular information literacy activity. Students are encouraged to engage with the information in a number of different ways as they work through their process using some or all of the elements. This model recognizes the importance of collaboration and so it is designed to support group projects and team working.

The InfoFlow model is designed to enable students to achieve the following learning outcomes:

- Learn how to work collaboratively in teams with other students and external collaborators.
- Develop metacognitive skills by reflecting on what and how they learn and how they can progress.
- Develop creativity skills by designing outputs which take into account the needs of different audiences.
- Understand how to engage effectively with a wide range of primary and secondary information sources.
- Learn to ask for, listen to, act on and give feedback.

Case study: The implementation of InfoFlow in information skills sessions

McNicol and Shields (2014) give a case study of the application of InfoFlow in information skills sessions aimed at final year undergraduate students at Manchester Metropolitan University. Previously, these sessions had involved demonstrations followed by hands-on practice and library staff thought that these sessions could be developed by providing more opportunities for students to reflect critically on the information resources and to allow more collaborative working. They redesigned the 'exploring and evaluating web resources' to include the following stages:

Task: Students use, evaluate and consider the application of web resources

*Students are introduced to a resource with a brief demonstration. They are then given time to **explore** the resource and consider its relevance to their own work. During this time students are encouraged to **collaborate** and work together as they explore and reflect on the resources. During the whole session, students may **ask** a librarian for further information or assistance. Students were asked to **reflect** on the resource by responding to a series of questions which encourage them to consider the use of the resource in their own academic work.*

*Feedback from the students was received using Google Forms and this was used by the librarians to **show** the responses to the whole class and these were also e-mailed to the academic tutors. This meant there was a record of the activity and students' responses to it.*

(McNicol and Shields, 2014, 32)

An evaluation of the pilot project indicated that one of the effects of running the 'explore', 'collaborate', 'ask' and 'reflect' elements concurrently was that the 'reflect' element was often neglected as students preferred the hands-on activities. In later versions of the course, the structure was changed so that there was a break between elements – time was spent on each element in a structured way, and this was found to work much better. Feedback from students and library staff was positive, and the library team commented:

> We felt it offered a more holistic view to the use of library resources. An important part of IL [information literacy] is understanding what resource to use when and although this is something we knew students struggled with it's an area we hadn't really touched upon in great depth in our teaching. This activity was a successful way to get the students to think about the practical application of each resource to their own research.
>
> (McNicol and Shields, 2014, 32)

A New Curriculum for Information Literacy

Secker and Coonan (2013) provide a new vision for information literacy teaching in the book they have edited, *Rethinking Information Literacy*, which is based on research supported by the Arcadia Project at the University of Cambridge. At the heart of their work is the model A New Curriculum for Information Literacy (ANCIL), which uses the following definition as its starting point: 'Information literacy is a continuum of skills, behaviours, approaches and values that it is so deeply entwined with the use of information as to be a fundamental part of learning, scholarship and research. It is the defining characteristics of the discerning scholar, the informed and judicious citizen and the autonomous learner' (Secker and Coonan, 2013).

This is a very broad definition of information literacy and, consequently, the ANCIL model identifies ten strands for the curriculum:

- transition from school to higher education
- becoming an independent learner
- developing academic literacies
- mapping and evaluating the information landscape
- discovering resources in your discipline
- managing information
- understanding the ethical dimension of information
- presenting and communicating knowledge
- synthesizing information and creating new knowledge
- understanding the social dimension of knowledge.

For each strand, ANCIL identifies the following features: strand content, learning outcomes, example activities and example assessments. Within each strand, students develop through four levels, or bands, which are key skills; subject content; advanced information handling skills; and learning to learn.

Secker and Coonan (2013) present a series of case studies, each of which is related to one of the strands and demonstrates their application to practice. For example, in the chapter 'Becoming an independent learner', the authors Walton and Cleland (2013), present an example outline programme for a module titled 'Research and professional development'. This illustrates how lectures and workshops on topics such as developing research skills, plagiarism and referencing, writing styles and introduction to qualitative research are linked to other elements of the module such as learning and teaching in higher education, qualitative research and quantitative research. The authors describe how they used enquiry-based learning, information and e-learning, and demonstrate the way in which this was built into online peer assessment activities.

Metaliteracy

The term 'metaliteracy' is used to describe a model of information literacy that integrates critical thinking and reflection in the context of an expansion of information literacy to multiple literacies and digital technologies particularly social media which enable individuals and groups to participate in knowledge production, sharing and dissemination.

Mackey and Jacobson (2014) provide a detailed account of the development of metaliteracy and the implications of this approach for library and information workers. They demonstrate the complexity of individual experiences as illustrated by Gardner's theory of 'multiple intelligences' (see Chapter 2) and the importance of recognizing multiple literacies, e.g. media literacy, visual literacy, digital literacy, information literacy and transliteracy. In other words, they demonstrate that learning and literacy take many forms and is socially constructed.

Metacognition, higher order thinking or 'knowing about knowing' is a key element of metaliteracy, which enables individuals to access, determine, evaluate and understand a particular resource, activity or process. This takes place within a digital landscape such as social media, mobile media, Web 2.0 and open educational resources. Individuals and groups are involved in sharing, participating, using, incorporating, producing and collaborating.

A case study on the application of digital badges in a metaliteracy programme is included in a later section of this chapter.

Additional case studies

There is an extensive range of case studies available on different aspects of digital and information literacy, a selected number of which are presented here. An excellent source of case studies is available at http://archive.lilacconference. com/.

Case study: Wikipedia as a vehicle for information literacy instruction

Todorinova (2015) describes a project between Rutgers University Libraries, OCLC (the Online Computer Library Center, Inc.) and Wikipedia, which enabled library staff to develop their skills as Wikipedia editors and to apply them to information literacy instruction. They demonstrate how Wikipedia may be used to demonstrate concepts such as:

- credibility and evaluation of sources
- the process of knowledge creation
- relationships between tone, scope and purpose of research artefacts
- participatory knowledge creation.

Todorinova makes the important point that as students use Wikipedia (even though they are often told not to do so), it is important for them to learn more about the encyclopedia and to use it in a critical and professional manner.

See Todorinova (2015) for further information and the full presentation (including sound).

Case study: Visual literacy as a key component of information literacy

Visual literacy is defined by ACRL as follows:

Visual literacy is a set of abilities that enables an individual to effectively find, interpret, evaluate, use, and create images and visual media. Visual literacy skills equip a learner to understand and analyze the contextual, cultural, ethical, aesthetic, intellectual, and technical components involved in the production and use of visual materials. A visually literate individual is both a critical consumer of visual media and a competent contributor to a body of shared knowledge and culture.

(ACRL, 2011)

O'Hern et al. (2015) presented a paper on the importance of visual literacy. They explore the ways in which librarians may use their professional knowledge and skills to give students and staff access to visual images for use in their learning, teaching and research. In particular, they stress the importance of visual images to students and staff beyond disciplines such as arts, humanities and media studies. Following the rise in digital media tools for developing products, such as infographs and e-posters, visual literacy has become even more important.

See O'Hern et al. (2015) for further information and the full presentation (including sound).

Case study: Collaborate to innovate

Logan and Groves (2015) describe an innovative series of events promoting the use of mobile technologies in support of learning and teaching. Staff at the University of Sussex Library worked with colleagues in other parts of the university, e.g. the Technology Enhanced Learning Department and the Careers Service, to deliver a Mobile Technologies Week. One of the aims of the enterprise was to break down and work across the normal boundaries found in a university. Sessions were led by library staff, technologists, academics and research students. The programme focused at developing digital literacies at all levels and took an inclusive approach. Themes covered included e-books, getting the most out of your iPad, collaborative technologies, technologies informing pedagogy, lecture flipping and the use of apps. They demonstrated the value of developing a cross-departmental collaboration focused on student and staff skills development.

See Logan and Groves (2015) for information on this series.

Case study: Situating students in the scholarly conversation: poster sessions

Vong and Lui (2015) describe the use of the new ACRL framework for information literacy as a trigger for re-imagining library teaching sessions. They used posters as a tool for teaching undergraduate students about research and the research culture. In addition to the poster sessions, students attended workshops on scholarly communications. They learnt skills in producing posters and about the research process.

See Vong and Lui (2015) for full information, detailed plans and a bibliography.

Case study: Blogging along

Stewart (2015) presents her work on helping art and design students to develop their information literacy and critical thinking in the creative arts. She described her involvement in a second year design theory and contextual studies module, which was part of the graphic design and illustration programme at the University of Cumbria. Students were required to produce a blog as part of their assessed work and to work in groups and critically review a range of sources, e.g. books, peer-reviewed journal articles, infographics, images, YouTube clips. They were also asked to write an accompanying critical commentary to their blog posts and to comment on each other's work in the blog. This project demonstrated collaborative working by library and academic staff, and the use of a blog to support assessed group work.

Digital badges

A digital badge is an online symbol used to demonstrate that a student has accomplished a particular skill or engaged in a particular activity. They are essentially online certificates, similar to traditional badges earned by guides and scouts for their achievements in camping, cooking and working in the community. A digital badge gives an image, which is likely to include details of students' achievements and a link to further information such as type of award, criteria for the award, evidence and issuer.

Digital badges may be added to an individual's CV or included in their online profile, e.g. LinkedIn, and they may be displayed on social media such as Facebook and Twitter. They are increasingly being used within colleges and universities as a means of motivating students and acknowledging their achievements (particularly outside their formal curriculum), and they provide a record which may be used when a student applies for a job (Hart, 2015).

Digital badges are frequently used as an organizational-led initiative and are likely to involve staff from across the institution, e.g. library and information workers, educational technologists and developers, careers staff, IT support and academics. Key decisions need to be made to ensure that there is a strategy and policy for the introduction and support of digital badges and their award. Resources need to be found to support a digital badging initiative. Examples include: Mozilla open badges (http://openbadges.org), Credly (http://credly.com) and Purdue Passport (www.itap.purdue.edu/studio/passport). Sometimes departments within a university set up their own digital badge system so that they can acknowledge their students' achievements outside the normal assessment and grading regimes.

Within the UK, the Higher Education Achievement Report (HEAR; http://hear. ac.uk/) is designed to give a single, comprehensive record of a student's non-academic achievements, including in their extracurricular activities, and to list prizes and awards, voluntary work, international work and offices held within the university. The implementation of HEAR provides an opportunity for higher education institutions to include digital badges in all departments.

Case study: Use of digital badges in information literacy modules

The University of Central Florida awards digital badges to students achieving more than 80% in their information literacy modules. Students who achieve this grade are sent an e-mail which acknowledges their achievement and enables them to go to a link and claim a badge in a fully automated process. Students may choose whether or not to display their digital badges. The system is completely separate from any assessed work and credit linked to the module.

Further information is available at http://infolit.ucf.edu/faculty/badges/.

Case study: Digital badges for open courses

The Open University now offers digital badges for free courses in their Badged Open Courses initiative (see http://open.ac.uk/). It offers 800 short courses on OpenLearn and the successful completion of a course, as demonstrated by an activity record and statement of participation, leads to the award of a digital badge. The purpose of this initiative is to help motivate and build the confidence of learners and to provide them with a record of their achievement. The digital badges may be displayed on the student's OpenLearn profile or on social media such as Facebook, LinkedIn or Twitter.

Case study: Digital badges for metaliteracy

A digital badge is an online symbol or certificate used to demonstrate that a student has accomplished a particular skill or engaged in a particular activity. Metaliteracy was explored on page 43. This case study demonstrates the use of a digital certificate in metaliteracy.

The university libraries at the University of Albany (http://library.albany.edu) use the concept of metaliteracy in their user education. They offer digital badges – or digital certificates – with the following names: Master Evaluator, Empowered Learner, Produce and Collaborator, and Digital Citizen. The website describes what is required to gain each badge.

For example, the Digital Citizen badge is achieved through demonstrating knowledge of information ethics (intellectual property and information use) and social identity (online personas and personal privacy).

Summary

This chapter explores the concept of digital literacy and demonstrates how library and information workers are engaging in supporting students' learning. Changes in thinking about information literacy have resulted in developing new theories and models, four of which are presented here, and case studies demonstrate their application to practice. The models of digital and information literacy vary in detail and the degree of emphasis they place on different attributes. However, they have similar views on how to enable students to apply critical thinking and reflection to their work in an environment that involves many different types of media and therefore literacies, and to work in a participatory and collaborative style using an extensive range of digital and other resources. The topic of digital badges, which may be used to validate a student's digital and information skills, is also explored.

References

ACRL (2011) *ACRL Visual Literacy Competency Standards for Higher Education*, Association of College & Research Libraries, www.ala.org/acrl/standards/visualliteracy.

ACRL (2014) *Framework for Information Literacy for Higher Education* (ACRL, 2014), http://acrl.ala.org/ilstandards/?page_id=133.

Bravender, P., McClure, H. and Schaub, G. (eds) (2015) *Teaching Information Literacy Threshold Concepts: lesson plans for librarians*, Association of College & Research Libraries.

Carncross, M. (2015) Redeveloping a Course with the Framework for Information Literacy for Higher Education: from skills to process, *College and Research Libraries News*, **76** (5), 248–73.

Hart, M. (2015) Badges: a new measure of professional development, Campus Technology, https://campustechnology.com/articles/2015/01/14/badges-a-new-measure-of-professional-development.aspx?Page=2&p=1.

Jisc (2014) *Developing Digital Literacies*, https://www.jisc.ac.uk/guides/developing-digital-literacies.

Josefsson, P., Hrastinski, S., Pargman, D. and Pargman, T. C. (2015) The Student, the Private and the Professional Role: students' social media use, *Education and Information Technologies*, 1–12.

Kutner, L. and Armstrong, A. (2012) Rethinking Information Literacy in a Globalized World, *University Libraries Faculty and Staff Publications*, Paper 10, http://scholarworks.uvm.edu/libfacpub/10.

Logan, B. and Groves, A. (2015) Collaborate to Innovate: developing a digital literacies programme for the whole academic community, paper presented at LILAC 2015, http://archive.lilacconference.com/.

Mackey, T. P. and Jacobson, T. E. (2014) *Metaliteracy: reinventing information literacy to empower learners*, Facet Publishing.

McNicol, S. (2014) *InfoFlow (Information Flow): an Integrated Model of Applied Information Literacy*,
http://e-space.openrepository.com/e-space/handle/ 2173/321756.

McNicol, S. and Shields, E. (2014) Developing a New Approach to Information Literacy Learning Design, *Journal of Information Literacy*, **8** (2), 23–35.

O'Hern, M., Jennings, S., Zhimbiev, T., Brown, V. and Hills-Nova, C. (2015) A Picture's Worth: visual literacy as a key component of information literacy, paper presented at LILAC 2015, http://archive.lilacconference.com/.

Secker, J. and Coonan, E. (eds) (2013) *Rethinking Information Literacy: a practical framework for supporting learning*, Facet Publishing.

Stewart, C. (2015) Blogging Along: using research blogs to tech information literacy and critical thinking in the creative arts, paper presented at LILAC 2015, http://archive.lilacconference.com/.

Todorinova, L. (2015) Wikipedia as a Vehicle for Information Literacy Instruction, paper presented at LILAC 2015, http://archive.lilacconference.com/.

UNESCO (2005) *Beacons of the Information Society: the Alexandria Proclamation on Information Literacy and Lifelong Learning*, www.ifla.org/publications/beacons-of-the-information-society-the-alexandria-proclamation-on-information-literacy.

Vong, S. and Lui, V. (2015) Situating Students in the Scholarly Conversations: poster sessions as a pedagogical tool for teaching IL concepts, paper presented at LILAC 2015, http://archive.lilacconference.com/.

Walton, G. and Cleland, J. (2013) Becoming an Independent Learner. In Secker, J. and Coonan, E. (eds), *Rethinking Information Literacy: a practical framework for supporting learning*, Facet Publishing, 13–26.

Zurkowski, P. G. (1974) *The Information Service Environment Relationships and Priorities*, National Commission on Libraries and Information Science, Washington DC.

4

Employability

Introduction

The theme of employability was introduced in Chapter 1 and this chapter demonstrates the many different ways in which academic library and information services are working to support student employability. It covers the following topics: academic libraries and employability, graduate attributes and working with students.

The library and information profession has responded to the increased focus on employability through a number of reports and reviews, for example SCONUL commissioned a review of the literature on current practice in the development of employability skills and the role of the academic library (Wiley, 2014), and CILIP published a report by Inskip (2014). There is evidence of changing and developing practices at professional conferences, e.g. see www.lilacconference.com/. Wiley (2015) provides an excellent summary of the current situation including a detailed bibliography.

In addition, the SCONUL Employability Toolkit (www.sconul.ac.uk/page/employability) gives an extensive range of resources, including a literature review and a series of contemporary case studies.

Academic libraries and employability

Traditionally, employability has been the territory of the careers service, but increasingly library and information workers are becoming involved in it as employability requires digital and information literacy. Library and information service staff support students (and staff) in the following areas:

- accessing and evaluating information, particularly online information, relevant to employability
- accessing and evaluating company information, e.g. in preparation for an interview
- finding and communicating with professionals

- developing their online identity and networking.

Wiley (2015, 72) provides a useful summary of employability and its relevance to library and information workers in higher education. She includes the following observations on supporting students' employability:

- Explicitly address employability skills in existing IL [information literacy] sessions (and their promotion) to demonstrate relevance to the wider institution and students.
- Seek to have a link on the websites of other university departments and services (such as careers and the Students' Union) in order to reinforce the relevance of the library's training to employability skills development.
- Be proactive about contributing to existing awards and training: make contact with other services.
- Careers and other student services vary greatly in structure and responsibilities: find out how they operate in your institution.
- Accredited involvement in a core component of the institution's skills award or employability framework is the ideal.
- Business and customer awareness and digital literacy are elements well suited to delivery by librarians.
- Find out what training already exists so that you can add to it rather than creating stand-alone content.
- Work with other parts of the institution to decide how best to market your skills and training (the name chosen for the individual training sessions is important).
- Opportunities to co-present with someone from a non-library background may result in a larger audience and advantages for both departments.
- Consider running training for colleagues in other services both to raise your profile within the institution and to increase the chance of working collaboratively in the future.
- Improved relationships across the institution help everyone, including students.
- Help to promote and grade existing award schemes, even if delivering training yourself is not an option.
- Universities will have an employability strategy and there may be a group you can join in relation to this.

Case study: Employability project at City University

Bell and Asman (2015) describe a project which explores how the library service can support students in developing skills for employability. Their objectives included:

- *to investigate some best practice in other universities*
- *to build a current careers print collection*
- *to produce an online Library Employability Guide*

- *to liaise and collaborate with other departments such as careers.*

(Bell and Asman, 2015, 72)

Their work involved the following activities: identifying how graduate attributes (discussed later in this chapter) align with information literacy programmes, exploring the use of experience-based design, surveying staff and students, and holding in-depth interviews with students.

As a result of this research, they developed and launched an employability guide (http://libguides.city.ac.uk/employability), produced using LibGuides software. This guide highlights resources such as social media, company information and study skills. The guide was developed with the help of students through crowd sourcing and contains resources suggested by them.

The library also developed a number of workshops covering topics such as:

- current awareness
- how to research company information
- how to build a strong social media profile.

In addition, the library collection was built up to include items on interview skills, job hunting and communication skills.

Bell and Asman (2015) state that the benefits of working on this project include developing closer relationships with their Careers, Student Development & Outreach Department, and enjoying the experience of working with students and learning about their experiences.

Graduate attributes

The concept of graduate attributes is increasingly used as a means of informing the curriculum and the student experience. Bowden et al. (2000) defined them as follows:

> Graduate attributes are the qualities, skills and understandings a university community agrees its students should develop during their time with the institution. These attributes include but go beyond the disciplinary expertise or technical knowledge that has traditionally formed the core of most university courses. They are qualities that also prepare graduates as agents of social good in an unknown future.

Bowden et al. used a spiral image to allow for potential discontinuity in the student experience, rather than suggest all pathways reflect a strictly linear sequence. A student-centred focus to the development of generic capabilities is an essential characteristic of the framework: it is 'far better to focus on real life experiences and on what it means to develop such capabilities within them. . . . We advocate a strongly student-centred process and argue that the responsibility for managing it should rest primarily with the student in a context of university support systems' (Bowden et al., 2000, 11).

One of the benefits of universities introducing or reviewing their graduate attributes is that discussions take place about the knowledge, skills and aptitudes required of graduates, including the role of digital and information literacies within these attributes. If digital and information literacies are accepted at university level they become mandatory for all courses governed by this academic framework. It is therefore vital for library and information professionals to engage with these types of discussions and development activities.

Case study: Evaluation of the Brookes graduate attributes

Oxford Brookes University introduced graduate attributes as part of its Strategy for Enhancing the Student Experience 2010–2015 (see https://www.brookes.ac.uk/about-brookes/strategy-2020/enhancing-the-student-experience/). They identified a set of graduate attributes for each of three communities of students (foundation degree graduates, graduates and postgraduates) and each set has five core graduate attributes:

- academic literacy
- research literacy
- digital and information literacy
- global citizenship
- personal literacy and critical self-awareness.

These have been contextualized as relevant for each discipline and are used to inform programme learning outcomes. Table 4.1 opposite shows graduate attributes of digital literacy and programme learning outcomes for Business and Administrative Studies at Oxford Brookes University.

This table illustrates how graduate attributes may be used to embed digital and information literacy in a consistent and methodical style across a university's portfolio of programmes from foundation through to postgraduate levels. It clearly links graduate attributes to employability and helps to ensure that they are presented transparently and explicitly to staff and students, and potentially to future employers.

Working with students

Library and information services are increasingly working with students beyond traditional support for learning and teaching, and in many different ways: as part of the student employability agenda, as a means of continuing to grow and develop their services, and in response to the academic requirements of courses, through peer learning schemes, students' work experience, student academic projects and student volunteering. These approaches are described below, and the concept of 'students as co-creators' is outlined and explored with a number of case studies.

Table 4.1 *Graduate attributes for digital literacy and programme learning outcomes for business and administrative studies (Oxford Brookes, 2013)*

Graduate attribute for digital literacy	Programme learning outcome
Confidence and agility	Make effective and confident use of relevant and appropriate technologies to enhance learning, communication and problem solving (international business management)
Searching for and critically evaluating high quality information	Evaluate economic and financial theories and interpret business behaviour through the quantitative analysis of empirical data (economics, finance and international business)
Reflecting on and recording learning	Adopt IT tools and digital media as appropriate to aid the effective communication and presentation of ideas, and as a means of disseminating, exchanging and facilitating the evolution of material for group-based tasks (business and marketing)
Engaging productively with online communities	Adopt IT tools and digital media as appropriate to aid the effective communication and presentation of ideas, and as a means of disseminating, exchanging and facilitating the evolution of material for group-based tasks (business and marketing)

Peer learning schemes

The basic idea behind peer learning schemes is that students can learn from other students as they are part of the same community, and this helps to facilitate the learning process. Many universities and colleges take advantage of this concept by developing peer learning schemes, e.g. peer mentoring, peer education and peer counselling.

Bodemer (2014, 14) quotes a book by Alexander Astin (1993), which states 'a student's peer group is the single most important source of influence on growth and development during the undergraduate years'. Bodemer provides a useful review of peer learning in the context of academic libraries and cites examples of its value in schemes relating to reference interviews and skills, and information literacy instruction.

The advantages of peer learning for students include:

- having access to help and support from a peer
- peers using a similar language to themselves
- peers having had similar experiences to them
- peers being likely to be empathetic to their situation.

The advantages of peer learning for peer helpers include:

- developing their knowledge and skills of information and digital literacies
- improving their communication and presentation skills

- developing their confidence
- developing their employability.

The advantages of peer learning for library and information workers include:

- having additional support in working with students
- increasing interactions with students and the possibility of learning from their experiences
- accessing new ideas, ways of thinking and energy.

There are challenges to establishing peer support schemes. It is time consuming to recruit, train and manage a group of peer helpers. As students move on to the next stage of their degree or into employment it is necessary to start with another group of students and to go through the whole recruitment, training process again.

Work experience

Library and information services may employ students on work experience for periods of a few weeks to a year and be aimed at students on degree programmes, or be open to all students. This form of employment is sometimes called a paid internship.

Students who are recruited for work experience are treated as employees and the recruitment and selection process is the same as that used for other members of staff; they are required to follow the normal policies and practices of the organization. They normally have an arranged programme of work experience, training and review to ensure that they benefit from it.

Case study: Embracing the student voice

In an article in *SCONUL Focus*, Oddy (2015) describes the approach taken at the Newcastle University Library for engaging with students through a paid work-experience programme. She identifies some of the areas of work that the students have contributed to:

- customer research relating to the refurbishment of two floors of the library
- follow-up programme of observation and focus groups on how the refurbishment was working for students
- promotional and customer relations activities
- other ad hoc activities including handing out promotional flyers and postcards; conducting quick surveys; recruiting, leading or participating in focus groups; conducting tours on open days; being mystery shoppers; and providing feedback on publicity.

Oddy (2015) suggests that this approach to working with students:

- demonstrates that the library is listening to students
- encourages student engagement with the library
- helps to get service enhancements right first time
- helps to build up convincing arguments for further investment.

She concludes by saying, 'Integrating student engagement into our strategic and operational service planning is not always easy and can require considerable time and effort. However, the rewards from investing in an ongoing and open two-way dialogue with students are far reaching' (Oddy, 2015, 33).

Student projects

In some library and information services, librarians and information professionals work in partnership with academics by providing live projects for individual or groups of students. These projects form part of the academic work of the student and so they are formally assessed, and there may be some limitations on the type and extent of the work that the student can do for the library or information service. Examples of different types of projects include:

- development of e-learning resources (education student)
- critical analysis of the marketing strategy and plan of the library and information service (marketing student)
- research into the use of social media in a specialist academic library (public relations student)
- development of an induction video for new postgraduate students (film student)
- research into the impact of an online searching course (library studies student).

Case study: Students as consultants

Thompson, Hunter-Jones and Barker (2014) describe a project in which library staff worked with academics who were delivering a module on market research as part of a number of business and management degree programmes. This module was underpinned by the concept of experiential learning and students worked in groups on live projects. The library staff identified 20 projects that could be included in the module, on topics ranging from noise in the library, to food and drink, social media presence, and perceptions of the library website. The students completed their projects, which involved following clear communication guidelines and channels with the module team and the library and information staff. Once the projects were marked the library staff were given the completed student work and they produced a report for the library managers based on the students' recommendations (which often matched their own thinking). The authors gave the following examples of lessons learnt:

- *Students from China were used to basic kitchen facilities in their library to prepare their own snacks and drinks and expected this from a library.*
- *There was demand for more visual content via our social media channels and less re-use of links and tweets from other university channels.*
- *Awareness of off-campus service is low.*
- *Students can struggle to find items in our libraries, and need clearer signposting.*

(Thompson, Hunter-Jones and Barker, 2014, 16)

Afterwards the students and library and information staff said that the exercise had been valuable. It provided an opportunity for student engagement and library and information service development, and enhanced the students' employability skills through participating in 'live' projects.

Student volunteers

Many universities and colleges have extensive volunteering programmes, which they run as a means of enhancing students' experience (and their CVs) and demonstrating their commitment to their local and/or global communities, and/or the environment. These volunteering activities may involve working with local voluntary groups, travelling to other countries to contribute to their projects and activities, or setting up their own social enterprises. Universities often support a volunteer manager and team who manage the volunteering experiences of students.

The use of volunteering within academic institutions varies and in part depends on the context, country and culture. Many universities and colleges have very clear policies about the use of volunteers within their organization and say that they may not be used for tasks which a staff member would normally perform.

In some library and information services there are concerns about using student volunteers (sometimes called unpaid interns) for the following reasons: the use of volunteers to potentially carry out work that is the role of paid employees; potential exploitation of students; many students experience financial hardship and cannot afford to volunteer; students' complex lifestyles (including full-time academic study, part or full-time employment, caring responsibilities, travel time) give them little time to volunteer. Consequently, many academic libraries and information services involve students in other ways such as in peer learning schemes, for work experience, to carry out fieldwork and to work on academic projects.

Case study: Volunteers in the School of History, Classics and Archeology at the University of Edinburgh

In a guest editorial on student volunteers in academic libraries, Forrest (2012) writes about her experience of working with volunteers in the book collections of the School of History, Classics and Archeology at the University of Edinburgh. She works with 20 student volunteers on a range of activities including cataloguing and the students provide valuable feedback on topics such as the use of space within the library. She emphasizes the benefits gained by using student volunteers and suggests that their use may increase during times of financial constraint. Forrest also explains how volunteering experience can be included in the student HEAR (outlined in Chapter 3).

Case study: Volunteer programme in a college library in India

Tikam (2011) describes a volunteering programme in a college library in Mumbai, India. The project involved 112 student volunteers who found the experience satisfying as it made an important contribution to their college library. They obtained attendance credit for the number of hours they worked (up to a maximum of 150) on data entry for a barcoding project. Students valued the experience and said that it enhanced their CV in preparation for applying to foreign universities or searching for employment. However, they expected more substantial outcomes and flexibility from the programme. One advantage of the programme was that it strengthened the bond between library staff and students and gave the students new insights into the library's systems and services.

Tikam (2011) provides a series of recommendations in the form of a model for working with volunteers, which covers the following topics:

- aims and objectives of the volunteering programme
- required outcomes
- recruitment and selection process
- training, development and support for volunteers
- conditions of services
- recognition of volunteers.

Students as co-creators

In response to a number of changes within the higher education sector, including its marketization, new ways are developing of thinking about and working with students. Traditionally, institutions 'listen' to students and respond to their needs but, as Dunne and Zandstra (2011) point out, this approach implicitly treats students as consumers. Increasingly, many institutions are now working with students as 'active collaborators', 'co-producers' or 'co-creators'. This is a radical shift in thinking and it requires a change in power so that students are active players in all aspects of their institution's life and work. This shift is demonstrated in Table 4.2, on the next page, adapted from Bovill and Bulley (2011), which lists a tutor's influence for different types of curriculum, and is explored in more detail in Chapter 5, in the context of changing approaches to learning and teaching.

Students may work as co-creators in a number of ways within a higher education institution. Typical examples include:

Table 4.2 *A tutor's influence on different types of curriculum and student's level of participation (Bovill and Bulley, 2011)*

Type of curriculum	Tutor's influence	Student's increasing level of participation
Dictated by tutor	Tutor controls all decisions	
Limited choice from a list of options	Tutor controls and limits decisions	
Wider choice	Tutor controls and limits decisions	
Students control some areas of choice	Tutor negotiates with students but has final control	
Negotiated curriculum	Shared control of decision making	
Students' curriculum	Students in control	

- as pedagogic consultants, ambassadors and evaluators
- as co-designers of the curriculum
- as co-facilitators in staff development workshops and conferences
- as members of a range of panels including student disciplinary panels, staff recruitment and selection panels
- as members of committees, panels and working groups associated with departments and faculties
- as members of research and other teams
- as developers of strategy and policy at institutional, faculty and departmental levels.

Case study: Digital Literacies in Transition Project at the University of Greenwich

The Digital Literacies in Transition Project at the University of Greenwich used a cross-institutional interdisciplinary, student-led research team, where students were both researchers and change agents. One aspect of the project involved the students working with numerous stakeholders, including employers, alumni, staff and students, through a process that enabled them to enhance their digital practice and skills. This included developing open educational resources (see Chapter 7) to support student and staff digital literacy.

For further information see www.DlinHE.com.

Case study: The Graduate Virtual Research Environment at Hull University

The Graduate Virtual Research Environment (GVRE) was developed at Hull University as a means of providing additional support to research students. Focus groups with research students and early career researchers showed that they wanted to learn about the research journey from other students and academics, rather than from academic journals and research textbooks. Consequently, doctoral research students were recruited as resource developers. This process was led by a project manager who organized the recruitment and management of students, who were paid for this work, and he also managed the quality control of the resources. The GVRE involved students as co-creators as well as users of the learning resources, and produced more than 250 video clips plus other resources. They illustrate all stages of research and students and staff at all stages of their research journeys.

For further information see Costello et al. (2012).

Case study: Students create learning resources at the University of Bedford

An innovative project between students in the Faculty of Health and Social Sciences and the Centre for Learning Excellence at the University of Bedford encouraged students to act as co-creators for e-learning resources. This was managed through a two-day workshop attended by students and staff, which resulted in resources which were then further developed, evaluated and published as reusable learning objects. The project was part of Steps, a university-supported initiative, which focused on student engagement.

Further information is available at www.beds.ac.uk.

Case study: Student library champions at the University of Bangor

The University of Bangor, Wales, runs a student library champion scheme whose purpose is to enhance student engagement and feedback, and to develop services to students. Each student on the scheme works with academic support librarians on small projects and co-ordinates student feedback. They receive training for the role, which involves one to two hours a week; the students are paid a fee for this work. The advantages for students are that they develop their skills, e.g. communication skills, teamwork and market research, which helps them build up their CV, and to gain points towards the Bangor Employability Award. Further information is available at www.bangor.ac.uk.

Further information on the concept of students as co-creators and an extensive range of examples and other resources is available in Healey (2013).

Summary

Graduate employability is now high on the agenda for many colleges and universities and this has had an impact on library and information staff in a number of ways. They may be involved in working more closely with careers and other professionals to support students. An increasing number of institutions have developed graduate attributes, which are likely to include digital and information literacy, giving new opportunities for librarians.

Increasingly, library and information services are working with students in many different ways including through peer learning schemes, students' work experience, student academic projects and student volunteering. These different ways of working help students to develop their employability skills and provide library and information services with new ideas and opportunities for learning about their students' needs. Finally, the concept of 'students as co-creator' is outlined and explored with a number of case studies.

References

Astin, A. (1993) *What Matters in College? Four critical years revisited*, Jossey-Bass.

Bell, D. and Asman, A. (2015) Employability Project at City University, *SCONUL Focus*, **64**, 72–3.

Bodemer, B. B. (2014) They CAN and they SHOULD: undergraduates providing peer reference and instruction, *College and Research Libraries*, **75** (2), 162–78.

Bovill, C. and Bulley, C. (2011) A Model of Active Student Participation in Curriculum Design: exploring desirability and possibility. In Rust, C. (ed.), *Improving Student Learning: proceedings of the ISSOTL/ISL Conference*, October 2010, Oxford Centre for Staff and Learning Development.

Bowden, J., Hart, G., King, B., Trigwell, K. and Watts, O. (2000) *Generic Capabilities of ATN University Graduates*, Australian Government Department of Education, Training and Youth Affairs.

Costello, R., Shaw, R., Mundy, D. and Allan, B. (2012) Tailoring E-learning 2.0 to Facilitate EU/international Postgraduate Student Needs with the GVRE, *International Journal for e-Learning Security (IJeLS)*, **2**, 3–4, www.infonomics-society.org.

Dunne, E. and Zandstra, R. (2011) Students as Change Agents: new ways of engaging with learning and teaching in higher education, University of Exeter, Escalate and Higher Education Academy, http://escalate.ac.uk/8064.

Forrest, M. (2012) Student Volunteers in Academic Libraries, *New Review of Academic Librarianship*, **18** (1), 1–6.

Healey, M. (2013) *Students as Change Agents*, keynote presentation to conference on student–staff partnerships: What is Partnership?, University of Leicester, 27 November, www2.le.ac.uk.

Inskip, C. (2014) *Information Literacy is for Life, not just for a Good Degree*, www.cilip.co.uk.

Oddy, L. (2015) Embracing the Student Voice, *SCONUL Focus*, **64**, 31–3.

Oxford Brookes (2013) Examples of How Digital Literacy has been Defined in Programme Learning Outcomes, https://wiki.brookes.ac.uk/download/attachments/120946694/Digital+Literacy+in+the+Disciplines+table.pdf.

Thompson, E., Hunter-Jones, P. and Barker, A. (2014) Students as Consultants: a fresh approach to customer engagement, *SCONUL Focus*, **61**, 14–16.

Tikam, M. (2011) Library Volunteerism Outcomes: what student volunteers expect, *Library Management*, **32** (8/9), 552–64.

Wiley, M. (2014) *A Review of the Literature on Current Practice in the Development of Employability Skills*, www.sconul.ac.uk/.

Wiley, M. (2015) From the Library to the Workplace: how information professionals can support the development of employability skills, *SCONUL Focus*, **64**, 74–80.

5

Approaches to learning and teaching

Introduction

In recent years, there has been a major shift in thinking about learning and teaching resulting in the development of new theories and models, which are now influencing practice in colleges and universities. It is a challenge to work through all the ideas and models of learning and teaching, and then to consider whether or not they are relevant to your practice. This chapter provides an overview of influential ideas and models relevant to supporting students' learning in higher education.

The main ideas explored in this chapter are:

- Kolb's learning cycle
- Laurillard's conversational framework for university teaching
- Entwistle's teaching for understanding at university
- Land and Meyer's threshold concepts
- the Higher Education Academy's work on flexible pedagogies.

The summaries below identify key points from each of these theories or models, which are very relevant to supporting student learning.

Kolb's learning cycle

The seminal work of Kolb still influences learning and teaching in colleges and universities. Kolb (1984, 38) suggested that 'learning is the process whereby knowledge is created through the transformation of experience'. Kolb developed an experiential learning cycle, which is illustrated in Figure 5.1 on the next page.

In a Kolb cycle a learner carries out a concrete experience, then reflects on the new experience. The reflective process produces new ideas, a new theory or a modification of an existing abstract concept. This leads to active experimentation where the student applies the new idea to practice. This cycle is often re-presented in a simpler style, as shown in Figure 5.2 on the next page.

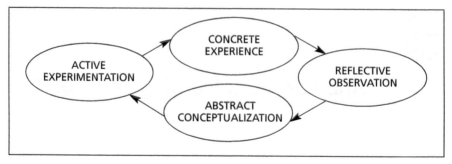

Figure 5.1 *Kolb's experiential learning cycle (Kolb, 1984)*

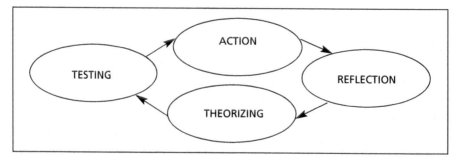

Figure 5.2 *Simple version of Kolb's learning cycle (Kolb, 1984)*

Kolb (1984) suggested that learning is a process which involves all four stages of the learning cycle: concrete experience; reflective observation; abstract concept-ualization; and active experimentation. This is often described as: action; reflection; theorizing; and testing. Individuals may have a preference for one or more of these stages, which he describes as their preferred learning style. Kolb's work has led to the development of different ideas about learning styles (see Chapter 2). Although some research literature critiques Kolb's work and subsequent ideas and models on learning styles, his ideas are still influencing teaching and learning in higher education. For example, Kolb's work is often included in postgraduate teacher training courses for teaching in higher education and they form the basis of approaches to learning and teaching, such as action learning and problem-based learning (see below). In addition, the recognition of the importance of reflection on action has resulted in reflective activities being developed and the use of tools such as learning journals and diaries (see Chapter 6).

Action learning
Action learning, an example of student-centred learning, is a process which involves a small group of people coming together and working on a specific problem or live issue. The process is underpinned by Kolb's model of learning. Action learning is often used as an underlying pedagogy for experienced

professionals who may be taking part in a master's degree or a CPD programme (see Pedler, 1996). The group may be self-organizing or led by a facilitator.

Action learning is real life learning on real problems, which may be complex and messy. An important aspect of action learning is that it is a structured process which involves reflection and learning from reflection. There are the following stages:

- Form the group.
- Decide on working practices of the group (how often they will meet, who will facilitate etc).
- Identify problem(s) to be addressed.
- Work on problems and at the same time reflect on the process and results.
- Develop solutions.
- Reflect on the overall process and outcomes.

The advantages of action learning are that it enables participants to share their knowledge and expertise, and to develop their problem solving skills and experience. It also provides opportunities for both group and individual reflection and subsequent learning. One disadvantage is that it suits particular types of problems, e.g. medium- or long-term problems, or complex problems. In addition, it may be time consuming and the outcomes may be limited by the expertise of the group (although excellent facilitation by the tutor should help overcome these issues).

Problem-based learning

Problem-based learning was first developed in medical education and like action learning is underpinned by Kolb's ideas; Savin-Baden (2007) gives a detailed description of it. It is a form of student-centred learning in which students work in groups of six to ten people facilitated by a tutor. The students work on a particular problem, which forms the focus of the group; problem-based learning is a vehicle for developing learning new knowledge and skills.

In problem-based learning students are presented with a problem, which has been carefully selected by their tutor or the facilitator. They work on this problem and share their prior knowledge. Together, they develop an action plan to help them to carry out their work. The plan might involve them working independently or in sub-groups, or making use of other resources, e.g. lectures, presentations or video clips. The tutor or facilitator helps to guide the students through their learning, which is sometimes referred to as scaffolding. The students come together at intervals to discuss and reflect on their findings, teach each other about their experiences, and work together to come up with a final outcome. After the initial team work, students work independently in self-directed study to research the identified issues.

Laurillard's conversational framework for university teaching

Laurillard (2002) explored the use of learning technologies as a means of transforming the student learning experience and she describes conversations as being central to the learning process. Her basic model is built on four components: the tutor's concepts, the student's concepts, the learning environment constructed by the tutor, and the student's specific actions. She describes a teaching strategy as 'an iterative dialogue between teacher and student focused on a topic goal' (77). This dialogue has four distinct stages:

- discussion between the tutor and student, including sharing of concepts and agreement of goals
- adaptation as the tutor adapts the learning objectives to the student's conceptions and the student integrates feedback and links it to his or her concepts
- interaction as the tutor creates a learning environment that is adapted to the learning activity, and provides necessary support and feedback to the student
- reflection as the tutor supports the learner through a reflective process to encourage him or her to revise their conceptions, and the student reflects on all stages of the learning process.

What is particularly interesting and novel about Laurillard's work is that she uses this model as a means of designing and using learning technologies to support student learning. She identifies different media using the following headings:

- narrative media, which are linear presentational media, such as print, audio, video, TV
- interactive media, which are presentational media, including multimedia and web-based resources
- adaptive media, which are computer-based and change their state in response to a student's actions, e.g. computer simulations, virtual environments, tutorial programmes, educational games
- communicative media via text, graphics, audio, video (or any combination of these media); note that social media have only developed since Laurillard wrote her seminal work
- productive media, which enable students to produce their own work, e.g. using paper, multimedia or digital media.

Laurillard (2002) argues that by matching the appropriate medium to the relevant stage of the learning and teaching strategy (discussion, adaptation, interaction, reflection) it can support student learning in an effective and efficient manner. As digital technologies are rapidly developing and changing the classification system of Laurillard begins to break down as there is a merger between different types of technologies. However, her work is still valid as it helps tutors to focus on the importance of learning conversations, and on carefully matching technology to the relevant stage or activity in the learning process.

Entwistle's teaching for understanding at university

Entwistle (2009) provides a critical approach to considering how students learn and why particular approaches to teaching and supporting learning are likely to be effective. He identifies the simplest forms of learning as involving attention, practice and feedback. He writes about 'meaningful learning', which takes place when a student takes in information and integrates it into a personal understanding. He considers how students learn both simple and complex concepts, and the gap that sometimes exists between a tutor's understanding of a concept and that of a student. He considers the important role of some abstract or 'threshold' concepts that need to be understood if the subject is to be opened up and the student is to develop their understanding. These are explored in more depth later in this chapter.

Surface and deep learning

Entwistle's research focused on how students learn and he suggested that as students become actively involved in their subject they move from a position of surface (or superficial) learning to one of deep learning (Entwistle, 2009). Surface or superficial learning is associated with rote learning and memorizing, e.g. last minute swotting for an examination. In contrast, deep learning is linked to students developing a much deeper and more complex understanding of their subject. By becoming actively involved in the subject and working towards understanding the meaning of the ideas that they are studying, learners are more likely to develop a deep understanding of the subject. Many of the learning and teaching activities described in Chapter 6 are designed to help students engage with their learning activities and move from surface to deep learning.

Academic understanding

Entwistle (2009) explores the nature of academic understanding from two perspectives: those of the student and the teacher: 'Students described their understanding in terms of meaning and significance, provisional wholeness (complete at that time for their current purpose) and irreversibility' (66). For example, some students wanted to understand something related to passing an exam or completing an assignment, while others had a personal need (or disposition) to understand for themselves.

In contrast, academics' approaches to understanding were based on ways of 'thinking and practising' within their discipline and this was prioritized over the intended learning outcomes of a module or course. In other words, students need to develop their understanding of the internal logic of a discipline and its threshold concepts (see later in this chapter) if they are to fully understand the subject.

Entwistle (2009) highlighted that different subjects and disciplines are supported by different learning and teaching activities. A simple example which demonstrates this point is that the discipline of architecture requires students to learn through practice and 'crits' – the critique of their work by their teachers, practicing architects and other students. In contrast, accounting students are likely to learn their subject through lectures and workshops where they spend much time working on practical exercises and receiving feedback on their answers.

Student-focused and tutor- or content-focused approaches to learning and teaching

There is an extensive literature on different ideas about learning and teaching, including tutor-focused and student-focused approaches. In tutor-focused approaches, the content of the course designed and delivered by the tutor is at the centre of the learning process. Typical examples of this approach include lectures and presentations, and some online learning packages in which students follow a predetermined pathway, which ensures that they learn a specific knowledge base. One feature of tutor-centred approaches is that the learner has little choice about what she or he will learn. This approach is sometimes used when the tutor is under time pressure (e.g. start of year 'one-shot' induction sessions) and wants students to learn about a particular service or resource. It is less relevant to situations where the subject is constantly changing and developing, and individuals need to deal with complex situations or conflicting data sets or information.

Student-focused approaches are concerned with enabling individuals to engage actively in the learning process and they normally involve real life and authentic situations. Two examples of different approaches to student-centred learning are action learning and problem-based learning, outlined earlier in this chapter. Many student-centred approaches treat learning as a social process and so students may work together in small groups on real life problems and issues. Typical features of student-centred approaches include:

- identifying the learner's starting position, e.g. their current knowledge and skills
- identifying their desired goals and outcomes
- real life learning situations, e.g. action learning, problem-based learning
- learning through interaction and discussion
- learning through independent learning activities.

Entwistle (2009) explains that this dichotomy of student- or tutor-focused approaches is an over-simplification and that many university teachers' approach to student learning is complex and likely to involve the following types of activities:

- importing information
- transmitting structured knowledge
- directing student activity
- encouraging understanding
- supporting conceptual change.

Supporting conceptual change involves a sophisticated conception of learning and teaching, and is likely to engage the university teacher in three different areas of activity:

- subject matter: showing enthusiasm for the subject and how topics relate to the whole
- teaching activity: guiding students' understanding and explaining ideas clearly and cogently
- relationships with students: showing empathy with students and understanding how students learn.

What makes a good tutor?

As a result of his research, Entwistle (2009) provides a summary for what makes a good university teacher and this includes the following attributes:

- showing enthusiasm for the subject
- being knowledgeable about the subject
- engaging students' interest
- caring for the students
- working at the right level and in accessible language
- making links to everyday life and experiences
- providing an appropriate classroom ethos
- supporting student learning through teaching for learning, and discussions
- managing uncomfortable moments as part of the learning process
- talking to students about their understanding
- supporting the development of generic and lifelong skills.

Overall, the work of Entwistle (2009) has had a major impact on learning and teaching in higher education. His basic ideas on deep and surface learning, and the extension of these ideas into a more holistic picture of the relationships between student understanding, university teacher's understanding, and the learning and teaching process has been influenced by the idea of 'threshold concepts' and this is explored below. Although he does not consider the implications of his ideas in terms of the discipline of library and information science he does relate it to many disciplines, including computer studies, history, economics, electronic engineering, and so it is well worth reading as a means of gaining a deeper understanding of knowledge and learning and teaching in different disciplines.

Land and Meyer's threshold concepts

Ideas about learning are constantly developing; a relatively new approach is summarized by the term 'threshold concepts', which have a number of features (Meyer and Land 2005; Meyer, Land and Baillie 2010). They are:

- Transformative: once understood a threshold concept changes the way in which students think about their discipline, or a particular knowledge base.
- Troublesome: they are often challenging to understand, e.g. they may be counter-intuitive or not fit easily with the student's current thinking.
- Irreversible: once someone has grasped a threshold concept and has a new perspective it is difficult to move backwards – to unlearn it.
- Integrative: they may bring together different aspects of a subject which did not previously appear to be linked.
- Bounded: a threshold concept relates to a particular concept within a particular knowledge base or discipline.
- Discursive: moving across the threshold may be linked with someone developing their language and a new body of vocabulary.
- Reconstitutive: the impact of the transformative and discursive aspects of threshold concepts result in a shift in learner subjectivity – a change in their understanding and a letting go of their earlier knowledge and understanding.
- Liminal: the state of 'liminality' occurs when a learner is stuck and attempting to understand something and may be oscillating between 'I know' and 'I don't know'. The 'liminal space' is where this takes place.

Summarizing and simplifying threshold concepts gives an indication that learning is often a messy business and sometimes individuals need to step into the unknown and let go of existing knowledge and skills. This is not necessarily a comfortable place to be but it is essential for moving forward. Meyer, Land and Baillie (2010) write about 'troublesome knowledge' and Shulman (2005) uses the term 'the pedagogy of uncertainty'. If individuals do not move out of their comfort zone they limit their learning and students may not achieve their potential.

The idea of threshold concepts is a reminder that all learners must pass through a threshold and once through this threshold they take on new ideas and perspectives. However, moving through the threshold is sometimes challenging and it may be characterized by an oscillation between 'I understand' and 'I don't understand' until the student crosses the threshold (or gives up and relies on rote learning). It is the tutor's job to help students across the threshold and to create learning situations where they will be faced with it.

Meyer and Land (2005) suggests that this movement across the threshold is not identified as a 'Eureka moment' but rather as a time when transformation takes place. Fister (2015) suggests that libraries and information services offer a space for this change to take place, e.g. through developing information literacy skills and providing a space where students (and staff) may engage with and evaluate relevant sources.

The idea of threshold concepts is changing the way in which library and information professionals are thinking about information literacy (for example see Hofer, Townsend and Brunetti, 2012). The concept of threshold concepts has been taken up by Association of College & Research Libraries (ACRL) of the American Library Association in its new *Framework for Information Literacy in Higher Education*, which is outlined in Chapter 3. A resource for teaching information literacy based on threshold concepts has been edited by Bravender, McClure and Schaub (2015). A general resource on threshold concepts is provided by Flanagan (2015) at www.ee.ucl.ac.uk/~mflanaga/thresholds.html.

The Higher Education Academy's flexible pedagogies

Recent changes in higher education have led to new approaches to learning and teaching, and one is sometimes described using the umbrella term 'flexible pedagogies'. The Higher Education Academy has supported research and development in the concept of flexible pedagogies and a key document, authored by Ryan and Tilbury (2013), and other resources are available at www.hea.ac.uk.

Barnett (2014) gives a thoughtful report on the conditions of flexibility in higher education and links it to the current context of living and working in a fast-changing, connected and complex global environment. He describes different kinds of flexibility: sector flexibility; institutional flexibility; pedagogical flexibility: and learner flexibility. The changes that have influenced these developments in thinking about learning and teaching are summarized by Ryan and Tilbury (2013) as:

- engaging students in their learning; this idea goes beyond having active and engaged students in the classroom to developing the concept of students as co-creators
- future-facing education: thinking about and preparing for the future
- de-colonizing education: thinking about and developing globally sensitive students and moving beyond an educational experience in which western worldviews dominate

- transformative education: an education process which goes beyond knowledge and understanding to the development of the 'whole person'; this is often linked with interdisciplinary and inter-professional learning
- social learning: using new technologies and social media as a means of developing communities of learners.

Two of these ideas are explored below as they are of immediate relevance to library and information workers who support students in contemporary academic libraries: the need to engage students, and social learning.

The need to engage students

Different models of learning and teaching, e.g. Entwistle (2009) and Laurillard (2002), highlight the importance of student engagement and conversations between tutors and students as an essential aspect of the learning process. Both models of learning offer a development from a traditional dichotomy of being teacher focused or student focused, to one where there is an important conversational relationship between the teacher and the student, especially focused on the student's developing their conceptualization of a particular idea. This shift in the relationship between teacher and student is illustrated in Figure 5.3.

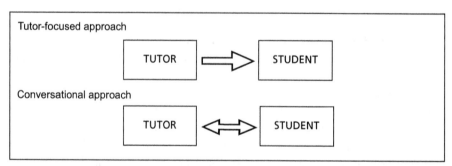

Figure 5.3 *The tutor-focused and conversational approach between tutors and students*

Within the concept of flexible pedagogies (Ryan and Tilbury, 2013), the idea of student engagement is taken further by developing the idea of students as co-creators or co-producers. The term co-creator is used here to describe students who instead of being passive recipients of an educational process are involved in all aspects of the educational process as participants and experts. Traditionally, students have been engaged in specific aspects of academic life, e.g. as course representatives or through Student Union activities. As co-creators, students are participants embedded in academic life and areas such as strategy development (Healey, Mason O'Connor and Broadfoot, 2010) or curriculum design and development (Bovill, Cook-Sather and Felten, 2011). If students are considered to be co-creators their relationship with academic and professional support staff in colleges and universities changes and instead of being 'consumers' they participate actively in a collaborative process of higher education. Evidence suggests that a key outcome of these collaborative practices is that they provide teaching staff with new insights into students' experiences (Cook-Sather, 2008 and 2011). The idea of students as co-creators is explored in Chapter 4 from an employability perspective.

Case study: Students as co-creators in a library space project

Ward, Hahn and Mestre (2015) provide a case study which involved students as co-creators. It used a participatory design approach in a project which aimed to develop apps to help students navigate their campus learning spaces and make contact with their peers. They used a competition methodology, which was effective. One of the interesting findings of the project is described as follows:

> One of the most important findings from the study was discovering a somewhat unexpected mental model for the library that the participants had in how they organized app content around courses, spaces, and people. While the grant team initially anticipated that students would design apps which focused entirely on library data (e.g. books checked out, hours, lists of study spaces, etc.), what the individual teams did instead was to organize their apps around the individual classes they were doing work for at any given time. This meant that the resulting app designs did not represent library spaces and services in isolation, but rather as part of an interconnected ecosystem that represented a student's daily scholastic life. The features in the design of many of the teams' apps thus focused on classmates, study groups, and timely data about resources and activity levels in the spaces these groups met. These components often combined in use cases to form an assignment level organization of content about both library and broader campus learning spaces.

This project illustrates the value students, as co-creators, can bring to academic libraries and information services.

For further information see Ward, Hahn and Mestre (2015).

Social learning

As Ryan and Tilbury (2013, 26) write, 'The idea of "social learning" is concerned with developing educational cultures and environments that utilize the power of co-curricular learning spaces, informal learning and social interaction in HE [higher education] experiences.' This theme is closely linked to the use of information technologies as a means of providing spaces for student engagement within the university setting. Ryan and Tilbury (2013, 26) list the key influences in this field as:

- scholarship in 'social learning' concerned with the social and cultural contexts and influences upon learning, drawing on thinkers such as Vygotsky, Habermas, Kolb and Wenger...;

- increasing focus on the personalization of learning experiences and maximising opportunities for collaboration in universities, in line with expectations around student choice and education quality;
- developments in thinking and new initiatives under the banner of 'café-style' pedagogy ... and 'free university' community-engaged movements in virtual and physical spaces;
- insights from critical theory, as well as practice-based models and experiential learning frameworks, to understand the situated nature of education as well as the influence of the 'hidden curriculum';
- recognition that IT developments seem to be prompting shifts of lifestyles, learning styles and thinking styles, towards more strategic, discovery-based learning but perhaps less competence in evaluation and critical appraisal.

(Ryan and Tilbury, 2013, 26)

This concept of social learning and its close connections with the use of information technologies has many implications for library and information work as it expands the boundaries of traditional learning spaces and helps to provide a focus on student-centred learning in the broadest environment (both physical and virtual). It is relevant to face-to-face sessions and workshops where supporting social learning, e.g. through discussions or group work, helps to facilitate the learning process. Online courses may include discussion groups, collaborative and co-operative project work. The use of social media to engage and support student learning taps into ideas of social learning.

The work of Wenger et al. (2002) is relevant here as it is based on the assumption that learners are social beings and that individuals learn when they make connections between ideas and experiences, e.g. through discussions and working with others. Wenger and colleagues developed the concept of 'a community of practice', which is a learning community or 'groups of people who share a concern, a set of problems, or a passion about a topic and who deepen their knowledge and expertise in this area by interacting on an ongoing basis' (Wenger et al., 2002, 4).

The importance of learning through different professional communities is explored in the final chapter of this book.

Summary
This chapter provides a theoretical overview of a number of different approaches to learning and teaching. These different approaches and models overlap, and it can be confusing to answer the question: what does this mean for my practice in supporting student learning? Below is a list of the key ideas for each approach.

This is the key idea relating to Kolb's learning cycle:

- the importance of learning through reflection on action or experience.

These are the key ideas relating to the conversational framework for university teaching:

- the importance of conversations between students and tutors
- selecting the appropriate media for each stage in the learning process.

These are the key ideas relating to teaching for understanding at university:

- Learning involves attention, practice and feedback.
- It is important to help students to develop deep learning strategies.
- Different disciplines are supported by different learning and teaching activities.
- Student-focused approaches to learning (rather than tutor- or content-focused ones) are important.
- Successful tutors have many characteristics.

These are the key ideas relating to threshold concepts:

- There are some key concepts which once understood transform a student's understanding of their subject.
- Learning is a messy business.
- Learning can be an uncomfortable process.

These are the key ideas relating to flexible pedagogies:

- the importance of engaging students, e.g. as co-creators
- the need to prepare students for the future, which is unknown and likely to be complex
- the importance of internationalization and enabling all students to have a global worldview
- the increased emphasis on developing the whole person
- learning as a social process and the use of new technologies and social media as a key element of the learning process.

References

Barnett, R. (2014) *Thinking and Rethinking the University*, Routledge.

Bovill, C., Cook-Sather, A. and Felten, P. (2011) Students as Co-creators of Teaching Approaches, Course Design and Curricula: implications for academic developers, *International Journal for Academic Development*, **16** (2), 133–45.

Bravender, P., McClure, H. and Schaub, G. (2015) *Teaching Information Literacy Threshold Concepts: lesson plans for librarians*, Association of College and Research Libraries.

Cook-Sather, A. (2008) 'What You Get is Looking in a Mirror, only Better': inviting students to reflect (on) college teaching, *Reflective Practice*, **9** (4), 473–83.

Cook-Sather, A. (2011) Teaching and Learning: college faculty and undergraduates co-create a professional development model, *To Improve the Academy*, **29**, 219–32.

Entwistle, N. (2009) *Teaching for Understanding at University: deep approaches and distinctive ways of thinking*, Palgrave MacMillan.

Fister, B. (2015) *The Liminal Library: making our libraries sites of transformative learning*, http://barbarafister.com/LiminalLibrary.pdf.

Flanagan, M. (2015) *Threshold Concepts: undergraduate teaching, postgraduate training and professional development. A short introduction and bibliography*, www.ee.ucl.ac.uk/~mflanaga/thresholds.html.

Healey, M., Mason O'Connor, K. and Broadfoot, P. (2010) Reflecting on Engaging Students in the Process and Product of Strategy Development for Learning, Teaching and Assessment: an institutional example, *International Journal for Academic Development*, **15** (1), 19–32.

Hofer, A. R, Townsend, L. and Brunetti, K. (2012) Troublesome Concepts and Information Literacy: investigating threshold concepts for IL instruction, *Libraries in the Academy*, **12** (2), 387–405.

Kolb, D. A. (1984) *Experiential Learning: experience as a source of learning and development*, Prentice Hall.

Laurillard, D. (2002) *Rethinking University Teaching: a conversational approach for the effective use of learning technologies*, 2nd edn, RoutledgeFalmer.

Meyer, J. H. F. and Land, R. (2005) Threshold Concepts and Troublesome Knowledge (2): epistemological considerations and a conceptual framework for teaching and learning, *Higher Education*, **49** (3), 373–88.

Meyer, J. H. F., Land, R. and Baillie, C. (2010) *Threshold Concepts and Transformational Learning*, Sense.

Pedler, M. (1996) *Action Learning for Managers*, Lemos and Crane.

Ryan, A. and Tilbury, D. (2013) *Flexible Pedagogies: new pedagogical ideas*, Higher Education Academy.

Savin-Baden, M. (2007) *A Practical Guide to Problem-based Learning Online*, Routledge.

Shulman, L. S. (2005) Signature Pedagogies in the Professions, *Daedalus*, **134** (3), 52–9.

Ward, D., Hahn, J. and Mestre, L. (2015) Designing Mobile Technology to Enhance Library Space Use: findings from an undergraduate student competition, *Journal of Learning Spaces*, **4** (1), http://libjournal.uncg.edu/jls/article/view/876.

Wenger, E., McDermott, R. and Snyder, W. M. (2002) *Cultivating Communities of Practice: a guide to managing knowledge*, Harvard Business School Press.

6

Learning and teaching activities

Introduction

Chapter 6 presents a wide range of learning and teaching activities which may be used by library and information workers as part of their face-to-face, blended or online courses or modules. This chapter is concerned with presenting basic ideas, common learning and teaching activities, assessment of learning and reflection on learning. In addition, it considers learning and teaching without courses, i.e. supporting student learning outside of scheduled teaching sessions.

Each learning and teaching course or event is likely to involve various activities and a general principle is to use a number of different types of activities as this will help to make the session interesting and engaging. The design of learning and teaching courses and events is explored in Chapters 7 and 8.

Presenting basic ideas

This section considered different ways of presenting ideas by tutors or students.

Briefing paper

A briefing paper is a short written summary of a topic with visual images. It is a useful tool for presenting basic ideas to students or as a means of asking students to research and report on a subject. It is likely to cover key ideas, present new vocabulary, and provide a guide to additional resources. Briefing papers are often used by tutors as a means of preparing students for their face-to-face activities. Students may be asked to prepare a briefing paper in advance of a face-to-face session or as part of an online activity.

Successful briefing papers are likely to:

- be short – no longer than four sides of A4
- be clearly written in accessible language
- define new vocabulary in a student-friendly style

- use images and diagrams
- include additional references.

Demonstrations

Demonstrations are a common method of introducing students to different resources. Their advantage is that they are a useful means of giving an overview, e.g. of a particular online resource. However, short demonstrations lasting less than five minutes are likely to be much more successful than longer ones as it can be very challenging to maintain students' interest in a demonstration and deliver one that meets the needs of the whole group.

Lectures

As with demonstrations, short lectures are effective in presenting an overview of a topic. If they are to last longer than about 20 minutes then it is worthwhile including one or more activities (see later in this chapter). Increasingly, lectures are pre-recorded and made available to students via the college or university's virtual learning environment. Therefore students can choose whether or not to attend lectures in person and they can access the same lecture many times.

It is standard practice to use presentation software such as PowerPoint in lectures, but there is a danger that this software is over-used – the so-called 'death by PowerPoint'. Increasingly, lectures and tutors are using music, video clips or interesting images as a way of helping students to settle down and engage with a lecture.

Lectures are commonly used at the start of the academic year as part of an induction process. In the US library and information literature, this is referred to as 'one-shot' teaching. Too often, new students experience a series of lectures in which academics, administrators, library and information professionals attempt to cram too much into very short time periods. In this type of situation it is counter-productive to present information which you hope will be remembered later on in the term. A more effective strategy is to put across a few clear messages in a friendly and welcoming manner; if this is accompanied by helpful images it is more likely to be remembered. A wider range of learning and teaching activities related to students' information literacy can take place later in the term.

PowerPoint and other tools

PowerPoint (or equivalent software products) is commonly used to support a lecture while it is taking place. It can also be used in association with a video or voice over to disseminate new ideas or concepts to students via the virtual learning environment, social media or e-mail. This has the advantage that it can be pre-prepared and released in advance of a face-to-face session with students or can be used by students taking part in an online course.

Jisc (2015a) provides an extensive guide with bibliographies and case studies on enhancing presentations using digital media and tools such as PowerPoint, Prezi and SlideShare.

Common learning and teaching activities

This section provides an overview of learning and teaching activities commonly used by library and information workers in supporting student learning. For all activities:

- identify a clear purpose or aim
- identify a clear learning outcome for the activity
- require an output from the activity either by individuals or groups
- think about the level of experience and confidence of participants
- think about how you will support individuals with additional needs
- think about how you will allocate people into groups (or let them choose for themselves) and the size of the groups
- think about how you will start and end the activity.

Action planning

Action planning often takes place towards the end of a course. At its simplest, it involves asking participants what they intend to do as a result of engaging with the course. Different ways of action planning include:

- sticky notes, on which students write what they will do as a result of the course
- e-mail or text messages, where students e-mail or text themselves or the tutor and identify what they will do as a result of the course
- sharing in class, when students inform their small group or the whole cohort what they will do as a result of the course. Sharing with the whole course often has the advantage that it helps to summarize the benefits and key points of the event.

The process of writing an action plan and then sharing it with peers, trainers or work colleagues can be extremely motivating. The key to a good action plan is that it should be SMART:

- specific: an identifiable action
- measurable: with something to see or hear that will show that the action has taken place
- achievable: manageable within the context of the course
- relevant: immediately understandable and pertinent to the learner
- time bound: with a deadline set or time allocated on a regular period.

This example illustrates how action planning can be used in physical and virtual classrooms.

Example: Action planning

A simple and practical approach to action planning is to hand out a sticky note to students and ask them to identify and write down an action they will do as a result of the training event. They can share this with friends or with the whole group. Finally participants can take the sticky note away with them as a reminder of their intended action.

Case studies

A case study is an example based on a real life situation. They are used to help enhance student engagement, encourage collaborative learning, and present complex situations or problem scenarios. Each case study is likely to contain the following features:

- a description of a real life situation
- necessary background information, facts and figures
- supporting materials
- questions to consider.

Sometimes, case studies may be very long, e.g. 50+ pages of A4, and these take a huge amount of time to develop and use in a classroom. However, short case studies can be used very effectively either as a means of triggering students' interest in a topic or in helping them to understand a subject. Students may be asked to:

- identify key issues
- suggest the best solution(s)
- reflect on their learning.

Short case studies are often a valuable tool to provide variety in a lecture or workshop and trigger discussion and sharing of ideas. It is important to make sure their focus is relevant to the specific context of the students, e.g. if I am working with nursing students then I make sure I use a nursing example rather than say a dental example.

This example illustrates how PowerPoint can be used to teach referencing skills.

Example: Teaching referencing skills

I used the following case study in a referencing and plagiarism session for postgraduate business school students. The case study and feedback took about 30 minutes. The case study is presented on a PowerPoint presentation with an accompanying PDF document. These materials were posted on the virtual learning environment four days before the face-to-face session.

- Please look at the PowerPoint presentation which provides a summary of referencing and its importance for your assessed work.
- After you have looked at the PowerPoint presentation, please read the three documents relating to the experience of a student, Jaafar, who experienced the University's unfair means policy and procedures last year. The four documents are:
  - the University's policy on 'unfair means'
  - a section of an assignment produced by Jaafar last year
  - a printout from the software Turnitin
  - a report from a tutor claiming that Jaafar has plagiarized part of his assignment.
- In class you will be asked to work in groups of three or four students and answer the following questions:
  - On the basis of the evidence presented to you, do you think Jaafar has plagiarized his work?
  - Do you think the evidence from Turnitin and the tutor is compelling?
  - If an Unfair Means Panel found that Jaafar has broken the university regulations with respect to this work then what do you think is the likely penalty (based on the policy)?

Discussion groups

Discussion groups are a useful method of enabling students to work collaboratively on a specific issue or theme. They may be used in face-to-face and online environments. If you are planning to include discussion activities it is a good idea to:

- clearly present the learning outcome, task, outputs and timing – summarizing them on a PowerPoint slide or as one message in an online discussion group – as this provides a useful reference tool during the activity
- require an output from the discussion, e.g. a summary on flipchart paper or sticky notes, or verbal feedback to the whole group; ask online groups to produce a list or summary in the collaborative learning space
- think about how you will divide people into groups and the size of the groups
- start the activity in a very clear style
- monitor the activity, e.g. by listening to the volume of discussions or monitor the postings online
- avoid interfering in the activity; let individuals take responsibility for their learning
- signal the end of the activity

- clearly end the activity
- ask for feedback from each or a selection of the groups
- give your own feedback on both the content and the learning process
- thank everyone for engaging in the activity.

Discussions may be used in face-to-face situations or in online discussion rooms or collaborative group software. The basic guidelines are the same whether the activity takes place in a physical or virtual space.

This example illustrates how a discussion group can be used when teaching students how to evaluate information sources.

Example: Using a discussion group in a course on evaluating information sources

A colleague described the following activity she uses when teaching information skills to final year dissertation students studying for marketing degrees. She provides students with a range of articles in both academic and professional journals that are relevant to their discipline and asks them to work through a series of questions on their own. Then they get into groups of three or four students, and she asks them to identify and prioritize their criteria for evaluating these different resources. Each group had to present their top three evaluation criteria to the whole cohort. My colleague found that this activity helped students to consider evaluation criteria in some depth and this helped inform their work on the literature reviews for their dissertations.

Games and gaming

Games are examples of structured play, which involve rules and challenges, and often collaboration and/or competition between players. The term 'gaming' is often used to describe playing games that imitate historical or other situations, e.g. Dungeons and Dragons. 'Gamification' refers to the process of using game design elements as a way of enhancing different activities, systems or services.

Smith and Baker (2011) provide a review of the value of games in library instruction in the context of college and university libraries. They state that games must reflect real learning needs with specific goals that are linked to the learning objectives. It is important to establish clear and simple rules. In addition, the games should be underpinned by sound pedagogy. Research by Tewell and Angell (2015), using pre- and post-tests, demonstrates that students in game-based information literacy classes did significantly better than those students who did not play games.

As with any learning and teaching activity, games require time to be spent on designing them, preparing learning materials, and testing them, e.g. with colleagues or students. If you are using a game as part of your course consider how you will manage the following stages:

- Introduction: set up groups; provide the necessary resources; clarify rules; answer any queries.
- Play the game: start and stop play; announce winners; give out prizes (if appropriate).
- Process the game: link to learning outcomes and give time for reflection.

The final stage is particularly important as it helps to ensure there is an educational outcome from the game as well as social and student engagement ones.

Jisc (2015b) provides very useful toolkits on the use of games and gaming, and suggests that potential users of games in learning and teaching situations should consider the following questions:

- What kind of game is appropriate in this specific learning situation?
- Is the game realistic and will it be accepted by the students?
- Is it practical to use this game in this particular situation?
- Will this game be acceptable to the students and other stakeholders?

Current practice in games and gaming is outlined below under two headings: digital games and traditional games. The Jisc Infokit on Games (Jisc, 2015b) has further information including the rationale for using games, many different examples, case studies and references.

Digital games

Following the development of an extensive range of digital tools, there is currently much interest in games and gaming using digital and online tools. Traditional games such as treasure or scavenger hunts have been adapted for use with social media, e.g. students post photographs of their finds online. Burkhardt (2014) provides a useful summary of the importance of gaming in library instruction and highlights that games are engaging, challenging and fun: 'Games let us practice skills like solving complex problems, collaborating with others, planning and learning from failure' (Burkhardt, 2014, 1).

Snyder Broussard (2012) gives a useful overview of online library games and critically reviews 17 games. She notes that they vary in quality and identifies some basic principles for developing digital games:

- Keep it simple.
- Work out a plan for using it in your course.
- Work out how to market it to your colleagues, including academics.
- Make it fun.
- Give feedback to the students.

Digital games are developing in the information literacy arena; examples include:

- BiblioBouts from the University of Michigan (see http://bibliobouts.si. umich.edu). This is an online social game that covertly teaches students information literacy and it is linked to them carrying out their assessed work. Associated with this project is an extensive range of resources on digital game playing. An associated resource is *Designing Online Information Literacy Games Students Want to Play* by Markey, Leeder and Rieh (2014). An interesting librarian's critical analysis of BiblioBouts is available at www.inthelibrarywiththeleadpipe.org/2013/giving-games-the-old-college-try/.
- Goblin Threat from Lycoming College (see http://lycoming.edu). This is a relatively simple game and at its core is a series of questions on plagiarism. In many ways, this is a quiz with gaming elements added to make it more fun and engaging.

As noted earlier, Jisc (2015b) is an excellent resource.

Traditional games

Traditional games may be used within courses, induction and other events within the library and have the advantage of not requiring extensive resources to develop and pilot them. Common examples include treasure or scavenger hunts, game-show-style quizzes and board games. One of the advantages of using game show formats is that the game players are likely to be familiar with the format and rules, and so require fewer explanations. Some examples are given below:

- Treasure hunt: paper-based – small groups of students are asked to find the answer to a series of questions.
- Games night: Blodgett and Bremer (2014) describe how their academic library stays open late one Friday a month for a games night. Table top board games are played throughout the library and students are provided with refreshments. It is a fun event used to encourage students to engage with the library and the library staff. It also produces a lot of good publicity for the library via social media.
- Large-scale, live-action gaming events: these may be used to encourage large groups of students to come into the library, work in teams and have fun.

Examples of how games can be used in academic libraries are given below.

Case study: Large-scale, live-action gaming events

Hubert, Smith and Lock (2015) describe their use of large-scale, live-action gaming events as a means of enticing new students into the library. They focus on two games (Capture the

Flag and Humans v Zombies) and how the library enabled them to take place. This involved marketing the games, working out the logistics, organizing music and food, preparing clear game rules, and ensuring that staff were available to support these events. They had to consider health and safety issues. Photographs were taken during the event and used for more general library marketing activities. Each game lasted about two hours. An evaluation of the impact of these events demonstrated that they were very successful and a useful means of engaging students and getting them to enter the academic library.

Case study: Play a game, make a game
Smale (2015) presents a brainstorming card game called Game On for Information Literacy, which has been designed to help library and information workers to develop games for information literacy and library instruction. This is a well used and tested game, and all the necessary materials are available to download, use or re-use from http://maurasmale. com/gofil.

Guest speakers
Guest speakers provide an opportunity for specialist input into a course and help to give variety and change of pace in a training course. The guest speaker may be physically present or visit using tools such as Skype or FaceTime as a virtual visitor. Inviting and managing a guest speaker involves preparation and planning including careful briefing. One method of managing a guest speaker is to use an interview format, as illustrated in the example below.

Example: Final year guest speakers
As part of a first-year undergraduate course on academic skills, I invited a final year student as a guest speaker. The format was an interview which lasted about 10 minutes and this enabled me to ask a series of questions about the finalist's experiences including his use of information sources. I also asked him to share his lessons learnt and to say what advice he wished he had received (and listened to) as a first-year student. I had briefed the final year student beforehand and had provided him with my list of questions so that he was fully prepared.

During the interview, it was very noticeable that the level of engagement and interest in the subject increased, and the students clapped the visitor at the end of his interview. The session was recorded and made available on the virtual learning environment for current students and a pre-arrival site aimed at new students.

Overall, it was well worthwhile using this approach to getting the message across. The final year student said that he enjoyed the experience and would include it on his CV.

Group work
Asking students to work in small groups is a useful method of enabling them to work together and learn from each other. It provides an opportunity to engage actively with the subject, and a means of managing large numbers, feedback and

de-briefing sessions. It also gives the tutor a break, e.g. from giving lectures or demonstrations, and enables them to work with small groups.

As with any other learning activity, group work needs a clear learning outcome, a clear description of the activity, a timeframe and a clear target, e.g. output or product. The activity needs to be structured so that there is a clear beginning, middle and end. These are some suggestions for how to organize group work:

- Start of activity: I always find it helpful to present the instructions on a single PowerPoint slide throughout the task. If students are not clear about the task they are likely to make up their own task or waste time by discussing matters not related to the session.
- Working on the activity: provide students with sufficient time to work on the activity. Give them time signals, e.g. 10 and 5 minutes before the end. Decide your role during the activity, e.g. do you walk around the groups and respond to questions or issues, or observe from a distance but make yourself available to answer queries? It is sometimes a difficult balance to find between giving support and interfering.
- End of activity: when the activity is completed, e.g. because it has come to the end of its time, then clearly end it. You may need to allow time for reflection (see later in this chapter). Complete the activity with a brief summary that links the activity to the learning outcome(s). Thank the students for engaging with it.

The production of a specific output or product is important as it helps focus the group. Examples of outputs include a list of key points such as advantages and disadvantages, a completed flipchart paper outlining the topic, being prepared to feed back to the whole group, and a presentation or demonstration to the whole group. Example activities for groups include:

- identifying the advantages and disadvantages of a tool, service or other topic
- discussing and prioritizing a series of topics, actions or priorities
- deciding on a particular course of action
- producing a visual image, e.g. a MindMap™ or spider diagram
- producing a handout, poster, guide or display
- planning an event or activity
- completing an exercise
- completing a case study
- writing a press release.

One consideration about working with groups is how to divide a cohort of students into small groups. There are a number of methods including:

- letting individuals choose for themselves
- allocating everyone a number or letter and asking students with the same number or letter to work together in the same group; different groups may then be given names, e.g. whales, dolphins, sharks
- asking students to work with three people they don't know or regularly work with.

Beware of the so-called 'death by feedback'. This occurs when a tutor asks everyone in a group to give feedback and the feedback is repetitive and long-winded. To avoid this situation, it is helpful to structure the feedback in some way. For example:

- One person feeds back from a table or group.
- Ask each person involved in feedback to make one point only.
- Ask individuals to add new points rather than repeat previous points.
- Ask everyone to give their feedback in no more than five words.
- Ask individuals to write their feedback on a sticky note and to post it on the wall or a whiteboard.

Here is an example of how a group work activity can be used in an academic skills module.

Example: Group work activity

The following activity was used with first-year undergraduate students towards the end of their second term. The aim of the activity was to help them to summarize and integrate their learning from the academic skills module. The task was to prepare a poster, video or blog on one of the topics covered in the module, e.g. referencing, plagiarism, information searching, evaluating sources, and the target audience was new students due to start the course the following year.

Students were given four hours of workshop time to complete the task. At the end of the module, the tutors (a librarian and an academic) arranged a social event for the students in which they demonstrated their outputs. Prizes were awarded for the best products which would be used to support student learning the next time the module ran.

Overall, the activity worked well. All the student groups completed the activity and produced a product. Although one or two students did not fully engage in their group work the majority of them were enthusiastic. They had heard about the prizes and the party from the previous cohort and were keen to be involved.

Future plans for the activity included using it as part of the summative assessed work in the module.

Ice breakers

As their name suggests, ice breakers help to 'break the ice' and relax people so that they can start concentrating and learning. They are particularly important if the learners don't know each other or are anxious about the session, e.g. during induction. Ice breakers are used to establish a climate for learning by helping to relax participants and enabling them to start to get to know each other, and they signal a start to the learning process.

It is important that the ice breaker used by the tutor does not cause individuals to be highly anxious or concerned that their time is being wasted, so it is necessary to choose an ice breaker that is appropriate to the group and the context of training, and ensure that the amount of time spent on it is proportionate to the time spent on the whole training event. For example, in a one day workshop it would be acceptable to spend ten minutes getting to know each other but this would be unacceptable in a short induction event lasting one hour. Here are some example ice breakers:

- Ask students to introduce themselves to people sitting at the same table or on either side of them.
- Ask students to introduce themselves and say what they want to get out of the session to the whole group. This works well when there are fewer than 12 students.
- Ask students to share hopes and fears for the course with another person.
- Hand out a sheet with a series of simple questions (six to nine questions work well). This is sometimes called Bingo. An example question is 'who had coffee for breakfast?' Ask the students to stand up and talk to others in the group until they have answered all the questions. The student who completes all the answers first is the winner.

Concept mapping, spider diagrams and Mind Mapping™

Using concept mapping, spider diagrams, Mind Mapping™ (invented by Tony Buzan, www.tonybuzan.com/about/mind-mapping/) or similar visual tools can be a useful way of asking students to summarize what they know on a particular topic. They may be introduced as an individual or a group activity, and students can carry out their work either on paper using coloured pens, or with the help of freely available visual diagram software, e.g. ExamTime (www.examtime.com) or iMindQ (www.imindq.com) and MindMap (www.mindmapfree.com). In addition, it is possible to obtain apps that enable you to create generic mind maps or equivalent visual representations.

One of the advantages of using visual diagrams is that many students find them very engaging (although in a typical group one or two individuals may not like them). Concept mapping and other similar visual tools may be used in teaching sessions for:

- individual or group brainstorming

- taking notes
- planning an assignment
- thinking through the vocabulary associated with a particular topic
- thinking through complex ideas
- working out logical links between ideas
- aiding revision
- presenting information
- summarizing information.

Posters, infographs and e-posters

Academic conferences regularly include poster sessions, which enable delegates to present their work in a colourful and imaginative way. Typically, printed posters are likely to be A1 size (the same size as standard flipchart paper). Increasingly, e-versions of posters are now used in learning and teaching; two examples are infographs and e-posters.

Infographs (or information graphics) provide opportunities for students to develop their digital skills and present complex information using graphics using a specialist tool (see for example https://infogr.am/). E-posters enable students to develop rich presentations involving links and digital media via a SMART board or large screen (see for example www.eposters.net/).

These tools may be used in teaching all levels of student; individuals or groups may be asked to produce a poster, infograph or e-poster and formally present it via a poster exhibition. An example of how poster sessions can be used for doctoral students is given below.

Example: Poster sessions for doctoral students

A northern university in the UK introduced poster sessions as part of their doctoral training programme. PhD students were introduced to literature searching in a workshop setting and asked to produce a poster that outlined their approach to searching and evaluating the research literature in their field. They were given six weeks for this task, which ended with a poster exhibition attended by academic supervisors, library staff and the students. During the exhibition, each student was asked to answer questions on their research strategy and information sources. The posters were assessed by their supervisors and contributed to their credit-bearing module on writing a literature review. Student feedback was positive and a number of them commented that they had expanded their searches as a result of talking to other students and seeing drafts of each other's posters.

Student presentations

Individual or group presentations by students are a common method of formally or informally assessing learning. Student presentations range in scope from a one minute summary to the rest of the class through to a 20 minute formal presentation.

The advantages of asking students to make a presentation are that it helps to focus their minds and organize their ideas in a logical manner. One of the disadvantages is that some students may find the experience very challenging, e.g. because they are shy or lack presentation skills, so special attention is required in supporting them.

When giving advice to students on making their presentation, I make the following points:

- Start by introducing yourself and the topic.
- Be positive and enthusiastic.
- Make eye contact with your audience.
- Don't read your notes word by word.
- Use a clear structure. A rough guide is introduction 10%, main section 80%, conclusion 10%.
- If you use PowerPoint display no more than seven lines per slide and no more than seven words per line.
- Use visual images, video clips (but no longer than a few minutes) and examples.
- Provide time for questions.
- Provide a brief summary, e.g. three key points.
- Thank the participants for listening and end the session.

It is also worthwhile encouraging the whole class to be supportive of their colleagues during the presentations and at the end, when ideally they will applaud each other.

Surveys and questionnaires

Surveys and questionnaires are extremely useful as tools for diagnosing learning needs, assessing learning, providing an activity that encourages reflection, and evaluating a session. They may be used in a number of ways and at different stages in the training process:

- pre-training session: diagnostic quiz and finding out about students' needs
- on the course: diagnostic quiz and assessment activity
- end of session: assessment activity and evaluation.

As with all learning activities, it is important to be clear about the reasons you want to use a survey or questionnaire. These are some important points to consider about the use of questionnaires:

- How do they help you to achieve your learning outcome(s)?
- Is their length appropriate? Students are bombarded with surveys and

questionnaires and are more likely to fill in a short one of less than ten questions than an extended one.

- Is their language appropriate for the participants?
- If you are using an online survey or questionnaire will you ask the students to complete it in class or in their own time?
- If you are using a paper-based survey or questionnaire consider how you will distribute it. Will you provide pencils or pens? Who will mark it?
- If you are asking students to complete it in class time what will you do if some people complete them very quickly while others take a long time?
- If you want students to fill in a survey in their own time how will you motivate them to complete it?
- How will you de-brief the questionnaire?

The internet gives access to tools that will enable you to design and deliver online questionnaires, e.g. SurveyMonkey (www.surveymonkey.com), KwikSurvey (http://kwiksurvey.com) and SoGoSurvey (www.sogosurvey.com). Many virtual learning environments also provide tools for carrying out surveys. Some interesting examples are listed below.

Learning styles quizzes

Ideas about learning styles are considered in Chapter 2 including their use in induction or orientation sessions. Online learning style quizzes are available at:

- Introduction to Accelerated Learning,
  www.open.edu/openlearn/education/introduction-accelerated-learning/content-section-5
- Index of Learning Styles Questionnaire,
  https://www.engr.ncsu.edu/learningstyles/ilsweb.html.

Plagiarism quizzes

Plagiarism quizzes are available at:

- Is it Plagiarism Quiz? https://ilrb.cf.ac.uk/plagiarism/quiz/
  (UK university example)
- What is Plagiarism at Indiana University?
  https://www.indiana.edu/~tedfrick/plagiarism/index2.html
  (USA university example).

Study skills quizzes

Study skills quizzes are available at:

- Study Habits Quiz,
  www.open.ac.uk/learning/induction/downloads/studyhabitsquiz/index.htm
  (UK university example)
- Palgrave Study Skills, www.palgrave.com/skills4study/ (publisher example).

Video clips and podcasts

The widespread availability of different technologies, e.g. mobile phones, tablets, cameras, makes it relatively simple to produce short videos, which may be used to engage students and add variety to either classroom-based sessions or online courses. The term podcast is used to describe a downloadable sound or video file; video podcasts are sometimes called vodcasts.

Typically, short video clips two to three minutes long may be used to enhance learning and teaching activities. Nowadays, students are so familiar with YouTube and the distribution of multimedia via social media that they do not expect top quality videos in their courses. These videos may be used in many different ways and produced by library staff or students.

Video clips made by library and information staff can be used:

- for a welcome from a tutor
- for library tours
- as a summary of key ideas
- in a demonstration
- for feedback on assessment.

Video clips made by students can be used:

- as a guide to the library
- for library tours
- in presentations, e.g. as a result of a class activity
- for students interviewing other students about their information seeking habits
- to give advice to new students.

Assessment of learning

Nothing we do to, or for our students is more important than our assessment of their work and the feedback we give them on it. The results of our assessment influence students for the rest of their lives.

(Race, Brown and Smith, 2005)

Assessment is a central component of academic life and used for a variety of reasons including to motivate students. It helps to integrate and consolidate students' learning if it is clearly linked to the learning outcomes of the module or course. If assessment is associated with timely and relevant feedback it helps to show students how to develop and improve their performance in future ('feed forward').

There are different approaches to assessing student learning and a useful distinction is between formative and summative assessment:

- Formative assessment takes place during the learning process and helps to inform students about their progress and prepare them for their summative assessment.
- Summative assessment takes place at a fixed time during or at the end of a course or module. It involves assessing student learning, often leading to a formal mark or grade.

Formative assessment is used to provide feedback to students and tutors while the learning process is taking place. It gives students answers to questions such as:

- How well am I doing?
- What are my strengths and weaknesses?
- Am I on track so that I will be ready for the summative assessment activity?
- What areas do I need to work on?
- How does my progress compare with that of my peers?

It gives tutors answers to questions such as:

- Will the students meet the course learning outcomes?
- What topics or skills need further work?
- How do I need to change the learning and teaching strategy and/or activities to enhance student learning?

Formative assessment activities may involve quizzes, peer assessment, preparation of draft or outline essays or reports, production of products such as blogs, wikis or learning journals, student presentations, or group work resulting in some output. Students may assess their own work or that of their peers. The results of formative assessment may not be formally recorded in the student record system although individual tutors may keep records as a means of assessing student progress.

Summative assessment activities may involve examinations, reports and essays; projects, presentations and group assessment activities; development of products such as multimedia, websites, blogs or wikis; and the use of reflective activities such as writing diaries or reading journals. Students are normally very well focused on their summative assessment activities as these frequently determine the final grade or mark that they achieve for their degree or affect their ability to progress to the next stage of their course.

Many library and information courses use formative rather than summative assessment activities, and linking courses to student summative assessment activities is a very useful method of improving students' motivation and commitment to their information literacy activities. Typical examples of assessment include:

- self-assessment either informally through conversations or more formally using self-assessment quizzes
- peer assessment, e.g. students assessing each other's work and giving feedback to each other
- tutor assessment, e.g. through quizzes and tests, or observation of online work.

As with any activity involving student learning, it is important to spend some time planning assessment activities. Developing these activities requires thinking through the answers to the following 'trigger' questions (Brown and Glasner, 2003):

- Why am I assessing?
- Is the assessment formative or summative?
- How is this assessment activity aligned to the learning outcomes of the course?
- What exactly am I trying to assess?
- What are the criteria for assessment?
- What is the level of assessment? For example, see Bloom's taxonomy in Chapter 7.
- What assessment method could I use?
- Who is best placed to do the assessing?
- When should I assess my students?
- How will I provide feedback to the students?
- What format will the feedback be in?

If you are involved in formative assessment you are advised to work through these questions to help inform your decisions about the assessment activity and process. If you are involved in formal summative assessment you are advised to follow your college or university's guidelines and practices relating to assessment. A useful resource is *Understanding Assessment* (QAA, 2012).

There are a number of online tools available for assessing information literacy:

- Information Literacy Test, James Madison University (www.jmu.edu/assessment/resources/Overview.htm)

- iSkills (www.ets.org/iskills/)
- Project SAILS (Standardized Assessment of Information Literacy Skills) (https://www.projectsails.org/).

These tests have been checked for reliability and validity. However, as they are standardized their flexibility is limited and there is also a cost involved in using them.

Here are two examples of assessment activities.

Example: Formative assessment

Bushra, a liaison librarian, lectures to first-year students on the topic of 'referencing and plagiarism'. There are normally 350–500 students in her lectures. She carries out formative assessment activities throughout the lecture through the use of an audience response system. She has a series of six questions, which she projects on the screen at different stages of the lecture and asks the students to answer. Their answers are displayed on the screen. This process enables her to gauge the students' understanding of the topic and she adapts her lecture according to their responses.

Case study: Making assessment less scary

This case study presents an example of a collaborative project, in which an online assessment tool was developed for undergraduate students to assess information literacy. Goebel et al. (2013) describe their work as part of the Information Literacy in Alberta Assessment Project. The tool is a post-test questionnaire, which is divided into three sections: demographic questions; a pool of 17 summative evaluative multiple-choice questions; two open ended questions. The tool was mapped to outcomes from the ACRL standards. They used WASSAIL open source assessment software.

The pilot project was successful and resulted in a further refinement of the questionnaire. The findings provided additional insight into the student experience and their knowledge of information resources and how to access them. The project team learnt about the importance of constant communication with each other, the project administrator and other librarians within their institutions. This helped to increase the profile of the project.

Benefits included institutions involved establishing a shared vision for information literacy assessment and this process was enriched by the different perspectives of members from different institutions. Discussions between members provided a greater understanding of the ACRL standards and gave opportunities for a more in-depth view of information literacy instruction in each other's institutions. Finally, the local solution developed through the project was very cost effective.

This is an ongoing project and the tool will continue to be refined and developed. At the same time, it is producing data which helps to document the current state of information literacy in undergraduates in Alberta.

Reflection on learning

Providing students with an opportunity for reflection is likely to enable them to learn from their experiences and may help them develop a deeper approach to their studies. However, it can be challenging to engage students in reflection as they may not immediately see the benefits. Some courses, particularly those linked to specific professions, may have a culture of reflection and students may be involved in developing reflective journals which are part of their assessment regime. On other courses, students may have little or no experience of reflection, and so may not perceive its value.

A simple method that I use for engaging students in reflection is to ask them to respond to the following questions:

- What went well (in the specific activity or whole training session)?
- What could be improved (in the specific activity or whole training session)?
- What have you learnt as a result of engaging in this activity or training session?
- What will you do differently as a result?

Depending on the context and the group, I ask individual students to complete these questions by using a sticky note or another method, or I may ask them to complete the activity in small groups of three or four students.

McNicol (2014) provides a useful list of ideas for reflection, which are presented in the context of InfoFlow (Information Flow), a model for information literacy (see Chapter 3). McNicol's ideas include:

- graffiti wall: asking students to write how they feel about a particular activity at that moment on a piece of flipchart paper on the wall or a sticky note in a designated area
- thumbs up, thumbs down, thumbs to the side: asking students to give immediate feedback on how they feel about a particular activity, e.g. confident, lack confidence, unsure
- headlines: asking students to come up with a headline in a very short timeframe, e.g. a minute, which sums up an activity; the headline may be sensational and eye-catching
- drawing or modelling: asking students to draw a representation of either an activity or their feelings, e.g. before and after
- using learner response systems: asking students to respond to questions using an audience response system or via their mobile phones
- video diary: asking students to record a video diary entry, e.g. on their mobile phones, and upload it to a designated site
- interview: where one student takes on the role of interviewer and interviews another student; this may take on the style of a chat show or news item

- thinking hats: based on De Bono's six thinking hats approach, where students analyse their work from different perspectives (positive, negative, creative, emotion, thinking; De Bono, 1985); this could be carried out by designating different parts of the room as a different perspective using a different colour
- stand in a line: asking students to stand in a line – a continuum – to show their response to a question
- if your group was . . . : if your students are working in teams asking each team to imagine that they are a particular object and to say what part of the object they took on in their team work, e.g. the object could be a car and the elements engine, wheels, steering wheel, clock
- group poem or song: asking student groups to compose a poem or song about their experiences
- group sketch: at the end of a long project, asking students to write and perform a short sketch, which demonstrates their experiences.

Additional ideas include keeping:

- a reflective blog
- a reflective diary or journal
- a video diary.

Learning and teaching without courses

In many colleges and universities, the large number of students and/or their distribution around multiple sites (often in different counties) makes it increasingly challenging for library and information workers to help support student learning in scheduled sessions. In this situation, the library and information service is likely to use a range of learning and teaching approaches to help educate students about their systems and services.

Common methods of delivering this learning support for students include:

- a pre-arrival website for new students
- websites with online resources and support, and access to online courses
- resources and support pushed via their modules and/or courses
- the use of a variety of tools such as apps, e-posters and infographs.

The following case studies provide examples of the different ways in which some libraries and information services are tackling learning and teaching without courses.

Example: Pre-arrival website

Study@WBS (https://sites.google.com/a/my.westminster.ac.uk/wbs-oer/) provides students with insights into business study skills and is organized into three areas: learning and teaching, academic practice and personal development. Each topic has a summary of points and video clips from current students and staff. Further information is available via a variety of web links.

It was developed in partnership with colleagues from across the university and links to a range of library and information resources including items on digital literacy and referencing.

Other topics include settling into your course; finding your voice; the UK marking system; and different approaches to learning and teaching, e.g. lectures, seminars and group work.

Case study: Freshers' fair

Baker and Warren (2015) describe changes in academic practices at the University of Chester including a shift from traditional induction process through to a greater emphasis on online activities. Library staff were concerned that they might lose out on face-to-face contact with students so they arranged to attend the freshers' fair. They established a working party, which identified the following objectives:

- to represent library and information science as a whole (including two fundamental IT elements: the University's managed internet access and mobile application)
- to be approachable, engaging and relevant
- to gain feedback to inform future years at the fair.

Using advice from other institutions, the staff decided that their approach was to be accessible and friendly, to keep it simple, and to give out freebies. They created an enticing presentation using Prezi (https://prezi.com/6zg6dntsdnam/uoc-mobile-app/), which was displayed on a plasma screen. Their freebies were put together in a student pack, and included:

- library guides
- a 'beer mat' featuring a quick response code to the library and information service website
- notepads
- a short quiz
- flyers for a library competition
- plastic card wallets.

The library competition, inspired by Pinterest, was called 'shelfie' and it involved students taking a photograph within the library and uploading it with the potential of winning print credit.

Overall, this new approach was successful. The following lessons were learned:

- Communication and teamwork are vital for success and it was advisable to make contact in advance with the Students' Union.

- Promotion of the services does not have to be limited to a single day or event.
- Freebies were important to make the stall appealing and attractive. Novelty freebies helped to engage student's attention, e.g. umbrellas and EndNote sunglasses.
- It is important to be able to calculate reliably how many students engage with the library staff at the event, e.g. a single core giveaway would give the potential for an accurate and measurable figure to record and compare each year.
- Know your audience and context, and tailor the approach to the students.

Example: Support for student's study skills

The University of Leeds Library (see http://library.leeds.ac.uk/) provides extensive support for developing student's study skills. This includes:

- Flying Start: a resource aimed at new students, which covers topics such as the first year, independent learning, getting down to study, and taking it further
- Skills@Library: guidance to support (one-to-one support and workshops) and resources (ranging from academic integrity to writing skills)
- Researcher@Library: advice and guidance for all levels of researcher.

Example: The Open University Library's information support to students

The Open University website (www.open.ac.uk) provides an impressive amount of support to its students, who study at a distance in locations around the world:

- online guides and handbooks
- advice to students with disabilities
- access to online training courses, which are recorded for future reference.

An example is an online chat session called 'The importance of being digital', a live question and answer session that is broadcast online. It is advertised to students as helping them to use digital and online tools and technologies during their studies, at work and in their personal lives. Students are able to ask questions during a live web chat via Twitter or by e-mail. As a trigger to help engage students before the event and to help them to begin to think about digital issues the Open University staff posted some trigger statements and questions:

- 'I've found an article on Google that I would like to read but I can't access it.'
- 'I've used information from a tweet in my assignment and I'm not sure how to reference it.'
- 'How can I protect my online identity?'

Additional learning resources include:

- Being digital (www.open.ac.uk/library/services/being-digital)

- An OpenTree adventure (www.open.ac.uk/library/services/an-opentree-adventure)
- Digital and information literacy for students (www.open.ac.uk/library/services/digital-and-information-literacy-for-students).

The Open University library site is well worth a visit as it demonstrates an extensive number of resources and support for students, and different methods of engaging with students using social media and other technologies.

Summary

This chapter provides a wide range of learning and teaching activities that may be used to support student learning in the classroom or an online environment. The different ideas are organized into four groups: presenting basic ideas; common learning and teaching activities; assessment of learning; and reflection on learning. The final section considered learning and teaching without courses through different approaches to support students' learning as an alternative to training sessions and events.

Chapters 7 and 8 are concerned with the design and development of face-to-face, flipped, blended and online learning courses.

References

Baker, K. and Warren, L. (2015) A Fresh Start for LIS Promotion: planning and evaluating our freshers' fair experience, *SCONUL Focus*, **64**, 34–40.

Blodgett, J. and Bremer, P. (2014) Rolling the Dice in an Academic Library: game nights help students feel at home, *American Libraries*, 1 December, http://americanlibrariesmagazine.org/wp-content/uploads/2015/01/1114.pdf.

Brown, S. and Glasner, A. (2003) *Assessment Matters in Higher Education: choosing and using diverse approaches*, Society for Research into Higher Education and Open University Press.

Burkhardt, A. (2014) Taking Games in Libraries Seriously, The Academic Commons, www.academiccommons.org/2014/07/24/taking-games-in-libraries-seriously/.

De Bono, E. (1985) *Six Thinking Hats*, Little Brown and Company.

Goebel, N., Knoch, J., Thomson, M. E., Willson, R. and Sharun, S. (2013) Making Assessment Less Scary: academic libraries collaborate on an information literacy assessment model, *College Research Library News*, **74**, 28–31.

Hubert, D. W., Smith, S. S. and Lock, M. B. (2015) Large Scale, Live-action Gaming Events in Academic Libraries: how and why, *College and Research Library News*, **76** (4), 210–14.

Jisc (2015a) *Infokit: enhancing presentations for the multimedia generation*, www.jiscdigitalmedia.ac.uk/infokit/presentation/presentation-home.

Jisc (2015b) *Infokit: games*, www.jiscdigitalmedia.ac.uk/infokit/games/games-home.

Markey, K., Leeder, C. and Rieh, S. Y. (2014) *Designing Online Information Literacy Games Students Want to Play*, MD, Rowman and Littlefield.

McNicol, S. (2014) *InfoFlow (Information Flow: An Integrated Model of Applied Information Literacy,*
http://e-space.openrepository.com/e-space/handle/2173/ 321756.

QAA (2012) *Understanding Assessment: its role in safeguarding academic standards and quality in higher education,* Quality Assurance Agency for Higher Education,
www.qaa.ac.uk/en/Publications/Documents/understanding-assessment.pdf.

Race, P., Brown, S. and Smith, B. (2005) *500 Tips on Assessment,* 2nd edn, Routledge.

Smale, M. A. (2015) Play a Game, Make a Game: getting creative with professional development for library instruction, *Journal of Creative Library Practice,*
http://creativelibrarypractice.org/2015/05/18/play-a-game-make-a-game/.

Smith, A-L. and Baker, L. (2011) Getting a Clue: creating student detectives and dragon slayers in your library, *Reference Services Review,* **39** (4), 628–42.

Snyder Broussard, M. J. (2012) Digital Games in Academic Libraries: a review of games and suggested best practices, *Reference Services Review,* **40** (1), 75–89.

Tewell, E. and Angell, K. (2015) Far From a Trivial Pursuit: assessing the effectiveness of games in information literacy instruction, *Evidence Based Library and Information Practice,* **10** (1),
http://ejournals.library.ualberta.ca/index.php/EBLIP/article/view/22887/17955.

7

Making it happen

Introduction

This chapter is concerned with programme design and development, which involves spending time thinking about learners and their needs, the learning environment and learning processes. These are some of the basic ideas that inform the programme or course design and development process:

- identification of the aim or purpose, learning outcome(s) and required level of learning
- design of structure
- identification and use of learning resources
- design of learning and teaching activities
- design of assessment methods (formative or summative)
- how to pilot the new programme.

An important concept is that of 'constructive alignment' (Biggs, 2011), which involves ensuring that the learning, teaching and assessment activities are directly aligned to the learning outcome(s) of the course or module. When designing a course, whether delivered face to face through blended learning or online, keep checking that the learning and teaching activities plus the assessment methods will enable students to achieve and demonstrate the intended learning outcomes.

My personal view is that time spent on the design and development process is essential if the programme or event is to be successful. Spending time on the design process helps you to think through the needs of the learners and their likely expectations, enables you to think through the whole event, and helps prevent you from making basic errors. Going into a training event with a well prepared programme and tested learning activities also helps to provide a professional impression, which gives confidence to the trainer or facilitator and learners. Finally, in the unlikely event that you are unable to deliver an event, then if a colleague is asked to stand in you will be able to give her or him sufficient information and learning resources to help ensure that it is successful.

This chapter is divided into the following sections: thinking about participants, basic design principles, levels of learning, basic design structure, design of individual learning activities, finding and using learning resources, reviewing the programme design, and marketing and promotion. Chapter 8 considers how to design face-to-face sessions, flipped classroom sessions, blended learning courses and online courses. The subject of evaluation of the impact of learning and teaching interventions is presented in Chapter 10.

Thinking about participants

Chapter 2 explores students' today and illustrates that we are working with very diverse groups of students with a mix of ages, previous educational experience, levels of digital and information literacy, employment experience, ethnic backgrounds and faiths (or non-faith), cultural backgrounds, financial situations, genders, preferred learning styles, disabilities or other special needs and caring responsibilities. Their experiences within the higher education context influence their expectations and within each higher education institution there is likely to be a difference depending on the home department, faculty or school of the student.

When starting the programme design and development process, it is worth finding out as much as possible about particular group(s) of students before you start working with them. You may find out about them by talking with their academic staff or professional support staff, or ask them directly through a face-to-face meeting, social media or e-mail. In some instances, it may be difficult to obtain this information but if it is possible to do so it will help in the design and planning process. For example it will help you tailor your session(s) to their programme of academic study, their interests and expectations.

Basic design principles

The starting point for designing your course or training event is to think about the students and to answer questions such as:

- Who will be there?
- What is their background and experience?
- How have they been briefed about the session? Are they likely to understand the wider context and how your session or course fits into their overall degree or other programme?
- What are they likely to expect from the session?
- What will they be doing immediately before and after the session?

In addition, it is worthwhile talking to the students' course and module leaders to find out their perspectives about the students' learning needs. Feedback from quality assurance and enhancement processes (see Chapter 10) also provide valuable information.

The next stage is to think about the overall purpose or aim of the session. This needs to be written down in a clear statement, for example:

- The aim of this session is to introduce you to e-books.
- The purpose of this session is to enable you to use e-journals.

This statement forms the basis of the design process. It is normal practice to identify a number of learning outcomes – what will someone have learnt as a result of this course or programme? Many universities or colleges use the phrases 'learning outcomes', 'indicative learning outcomes' and 'intended learning outcomes'. Occasionally they may be referred to as 'benefits of taking this course'.

Example: Learning outcomes

The following list shows typical learning outcomes for students who engage in a learning and teaching activity:

- accurately reference your work using the Harvard method
- list the benefits of planning an online search
- critically evaluate a selection of online databases relevant to your discipline.

Case study: Redeveloping a course with the Framework for Information Literacy for Higher Education

Carncross (2015) provides a detailed account of how she redeveloped an academic research skills module to take into account the new ACRL *Framework for Information Literacy for Higher Education* (ACRL, 2014). This is considered in more detail in Chapter 3. She illustrates the impact of the difference between the old ACRL standards and the new Framework using the following process.

Her first step was to review the old learning outcomes and re-write them (if required) to meet the new framework. She presented a table summarizing her work (see Table 7.1), which illustrates the difference between the two approaches. The case study demonstrates an approach to devising learning objectives using two different under-pinning models.

Table 7.1 *Example of re-written learning objectives informed by a framework (Carncross, 2015)*

Old objectives (informed by standards)	Revised objectives (informed by a framework)
Identify appropriate tools and sources to answer research questions	Identify contextually appropriate tools and resources to answer research questions
Weave new information into the student's knowledge structure in order to create a scholarly product	Contribute to ongoing scholarly conversation

Levels of learning

When you are developing a new course, consider the level of learning that you hope to achieve. A useful approach to thinking about this is to use Bloom's taxonomy of learning (Bloom, 1956), which provides a framework for understanding the different levels of learning achieved within a training session. The outline presented here is a simplified overview and some of Bloom's original language has been changed to make it more accessible. Bloom's taxonomy gives an insight into the different levels of learning, from being able to remember something as demonstrated by being able to list or describe it, through to evaluating it or creating something new. This is illustrated in Table 7.2, which shows the six levels of cognition and their relationship to a learner's achievements, together with typical learning activities.

Table 7.2 *The application of Bloom's taxonomy of learning in practice (Bloom, 1956)*

Levels of cognition	Learner is able to:	Example application	Example learning activities
1 Remember	Remember, list, define, describe	Describe the layout of the library	Tour Treasure hunt
2 Understand	Explain, summarize, rephrase	Explain why referencing is important for lawyer students	Lecture Podcast Study guide
3 Application	Use learning in new or different situations, implement	Use Boolean logic in a different online search	Demonstration Hands-on session Worked example
4 Analysis	Compare, organize, de-construct	Compare and contrast two information sources	Practical exercise Discussion Production of a report
5 Evaluation	Judges, sets and uses criteria to evaluate; prioritizes	Evaluate the relevance of a learning resource for a particular group of learners	Practical activity Produce a poster Discussion Reflection
6 Creation	Design, build, construct, produce	Write an evidence-based literature review	Independent learning, e.g. project work

---

Example: Linking learning outcomes to Bloom's taxonomy

This example illustrates how learning outcomes are written in line with the different levels of learning identified in Bloom's taxonomy. These are the learning outcomes, each of which is linked to one of the levels of Bloom's taxonomy, as illustrated in Table 7.2.

- By the end of the training event, delegates will be able to find and use e-journals (Level 1).

- As a result of engaging in the workshop, students will be able to explain the academic consequences of plagiarism (Level 2).
- By the end of the workshop, students will be able to search Medline using its advanced features (Level 3).
- By the end of the training event, students will be able to compare and contrast two business databases (Level 4).
- By the end of the module, students will be able to evaluate a specific database suitable for their specific research query and its context (Level 5).
- By the end of the module, doctoral students will be able to write an evidence-based literature review and identify gaps in current knowledge (Level 6).

How does Bloom's taxonomy connect to learning at the different levels within an undergraduate or postgraduate degree? It would be incorrect to think that the initial stages or years of higher education focus on the lowest levels of Bloom's taxonomy. At any stage from foundation year through to a master's degree, students may be involved in working through a number of different levels of cognition. In their first year, they may be asked to understand a new concept and to evaluate it in the context of a particular situation or problem. Some concepts are too challenging for students at the start of their degree programme and they may be left to the later stages of their degree when they have acquired a more sophisticated understanding of their discipline.

A useful resource on higher education and Bloom's taxonomy is available from the Higher Education Academy (www.heacademy.ac.uk).

Basic design structure

There are a number of different ways of designing the structure of a course. Basically, every course (face to face, online or blended) needs a clear and logical structure, which helps students to understand where they are within their learning journey. The simplest structure involves three parts, as shown in Figure 7.1 on the next page, the type of structure that most students expect. However, this is an over-simplistic illustration and a more detailed approach helps the tutor to structure and organize their courses.

Although there is now detailed debate about the validity of models and theories of learning styles (see Chapters 2 and 5), the Honey and Mumford model of learning styles provides some insights into the design of learning and teaching sessions. This is sometimes called the 4MAT approach (e.g. by McCarthy and McCarthy, 2005) and it is summarized below. I regularly use this approach in my training practice and have adapted this method to include assessment activities at specific stages in the design process. The reason for this adaptation of the model is that the original model does not consider formative assessment of learning; this is so vital, particularly within an academic context, that I inserted it into my practice a number of years ago.

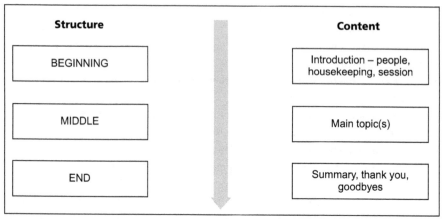

Figure 7.1 *A simple structure for a course*

The 4MAT structure is based on ideas of learning styles and suggests that there are four elements that need to be covered in any training:

- **why** the participant needs to achieve the learning outcomes – why they will benefit from engaging in the session
- **what** the participant will learn – the basic ideas or content
- **how** the material covered in the session applies to practice
- the opportunity to ask '**what if**' questions, which are often used as an opportunity to relate students' learning to their own particular situation, e.g. a forthcoming assessment activity on their course.

These four concepts form the basis of the 4MAT approach and they need to be enhanced through the addition of four elements:

- introductions
- formative assessment of the content – basic ideas covered in the **what** part of the session
- formative assessment of the application of the ideas (delivered as part of the **how**)
- time to summarize and close the session.

This gives the following structure:

- **Introductions** – these allow individuals to settle down and get ready to learn.
- Core format:
  - **Benefits** – these help to convince individuals that they will benefit from engaging with the session. Examples of benefits include saving time,

finding up-to-date materials to help them do their job or assignments, and preventing them from accidentally plagiarizing something. This is equivalent to the **why** in the Honey and Mumford learning styles model and meets the learning style preference of reflectors.

— **Introduction to the main topic: what** – meets learning style preference of theorists. A formative assessment activity may be included.
— **Practical activity: how** – meets learning style preference of activists. A formative assessment activity may be included.
— **Any questions: what if** – meets learning style preference of pragmatists.
- The **summary or conclusion** helps to remind individuals of what they have gained from the session.
- **Closing the session** in a professional manner helps everyone to know that it has ended and to move on to the next activity in their diary.

The pro-forma presented in Figure 7.2 may be used for designing courses, workshops and individual teaching sessions. Examples of application of the 4MAT approach to face-to-face (including the flipped classroom approach), blended and online courses are given in the next chapter.

Title			
Aim or purpose			
Learning outcome(s)			
Resources required			
4MAT approach	**Topic**	**Tutor activity**	**Student activity**
Introduction			
Why			
What including formative assessment			
How including formative assessment			
What if			
Close course			

Figure 7.2 *Pro-forma for planning courses, workshops and individual learning and teaching sessions*

Design of individual learning activities

As with the design of a whole course or programme, specific activities need to be carefully planned and the 4MAT approach works well in designing specific activities. Again, it is important to ensure that you have constructive alignment between the learning outcome(s), the actual activity and any assessment activities.

Chapter 6 provides examples of many learning and teaching activities commonly used by library and information workers. Figure 7.3 shows a pro-forma for the design of specific learning activities; this is a minor adaptation of the form presented for designing the overall course, session or workshop.

The value of using the pro-forma illustrated in Figure 7.3 is that it enables you to see at a glance what students and tutors are doing and if there is too much repetition in either of the columns, tutor activity or student activity, you may want to consider providing more variety. Once you have designed the specific learning and teaching activity it is worthwhile piloting it with colleagues, as this helps to ensure its success the first time you use it.

Title			
Aim or purpose			
Learning outcome(s)			
Resources required			
4MAT approach	**Topic**	**Tutor activity**	**Student activity**
Introduction			
Why			
What including formative assessment			
How including formative assessment			
What if			
Close activity			

Figure 7.3 *Pro-forma for planning individual learning and teaching activities*

Finding and using learning resources

Open education resources are learning and teaching materials in any medium that are available in the public domain and may have been released under an open licence. Increasingly, universities and colleges are sharing their learning and teaching materials, and there is now an extensive range of available resources. This permits individual academics and tutors to 'pick and mix' from existing resources rather than develop their own from the beginning.

The advantages of open educational resources (OERs) include:

- access to an extensive number of learning, teaching and assessment resources
- opportunities to learn from the practice of others
- opportunities to raise individual, team and institutional profiles through developing OERs
- opportunities to provide variety in your course
- being free!

Disadvantages of open educational resources include:

- time taken to identify and review potentially useful open educational resources
- language, content and approach not always 100% aligned to the aim of the course
- lack of quality control.

It is a considerable challenge to keep up to date with all the resources available for learning and teaching. This section introduces some key websites that provide teaching resources. Some of the resources have open licences, so they may be adapted and re-used in your training programmes. Others have restricted access but they can often still be used to signpost participants to specific materials. Table 7.3 on the next page gives a summary of useful resources for learning and teaching.

Reviewing the programme design

Once you have completed the design of your course and all the individual learning activities it is worthwhile considering the likely flow of events and the learner experience. The following questions can facilitate this process:

- Will learners know what is happening throughout the event? Is it well signposted? Will they know why they are doing particular activities?
- Have you achieved constructive alignment between learning and teaching activities, assessment activities and learning outcomes?
- Is there a range of activities including:
  — tutor or other expert input?
  — individual participant activity?
  — hands-on activity?

Table 7.3 *Useful resources for learning and teaching*

ALA website	American Library Association's website has a section on teaching and learning, which provides access to an extensive range of resources. www.ala.org/
CILIP's Information Literacy Group website	This site provides an extensive range of resources for information professionals on information and digital literacy. www.informationliteracy.org.uk/
Creative Commons search website	This site enables you to search an extensive range of sources to find openly licensed teaching material. http://search.creativecommons.org/
Flickr Creative Commons website	Flickr is a popular source of images. Using its Creative Commons search enables you to find material that you may re-use safely. https://www.flickr.com/creativecommons
Jisc digital media website	This colourful site provides access to information and advice on creating, finding and using digital images in UK higher education. www.jiscdigitalmedia.ac.uk/
Jorum website	This is a UK Jisc-funded repository, which hosts teaching resources from Jisc projects and other freely available material. It provides access to resources for higher and further education and skills, including information and digital literacy skills. www.jorum.ac.uk/
LOEX website	LOEX is a self-supporting, non-profit educational clearinghouse for library instruction and information literacy information. www.loex.org/
MERLOT website	This is a well established US-based site that provides links to teaching material for all subjects including library and information science. www.merlot.org/merlot/index.htm
NDLR website	National Digital Learning Resources (NDLR) is a collaborative community of higher education academics in Ireland who are interested in developing and sharing digital teaching resources and promoting a new teaching and learning culture. www.ndlr.ie/
OER Commons website	This site provides access to learning and teaching materials that have Creative Commons licences attached. https://www.oercommons.org/
PRIMO website	This US-based initiative hosts links to peer-reviewed teaching material for information literacy. Resources included in the database come from across the world and are peer reviewed. http://primodb.org/

— group activity?
— different media: print, visuals, sound discussions?
— opportunities for informal assessment of learning, e.g. self-assessment, peer assessment, tutor assessment?
• What is the balance between input and activity? Is this appropriate? How are participants likely to respond to this particular balance?
• How will the event be paced? Will there be time for fast and slower paced activities?
• How will you ensure that everyone keeps up with the course? What

happens if individual participants do not complete their activity within the specified time? How will you deal with it?
- Are you attempting to do too much in the allocated time? Sometimes, the adage 'less is more' is very relevant to the design of programmes and courses.

Marketing and promotion

Marketing and promoting learning and teaching courses and activities involves communicating and convincing students and colleagues about an event or workshop. Clow and Baack (2007) provide a hierarchy of effects model, which gives an insight into students' thinking processes about new products or services. There are a number of stages:

- awareness
- knowledge
- liking
- preference
- conviction
- sign up and attendance.

Marketing and promotion to students can be a challenge. It is simpler if the learning and teaching event is scheduled as part of a module but even then it can be a challenge to get full attendance. In addition, students are often bombarded with information and it can be a difficult to get your message to them. The following tools are commonly used:

- apps
- engaging e-mails, which include colour and images, including links to video clips
- social media tools, e.g. a library Facebook site, Twitter, Instagram, blogs
- video clips, e.g. a one- or two-minute long video made using a mobile phone and featuring a student or lecturer talking about the value of the session; these may be disseminated via social media or e-mail
- infographics: visually exciting charts and posters, which may be disseminated in print or electronically (e.g. see https://infogr.am/)
- e-posters: posted in learning and social spaces using a SMART board or a large monitor and computer to display the poster and give access to its resources; they are visually attractive and so likely to be of interest to students.

A very important source of help for communicating and promoting learning and teaching activities is through other people, including:

- module leaders and course leaders

- student support staff, e.g. in faculty student support offices
- student ambassadors, representatives and other students working in partnership with the library and information service
- the Students' Union.

Case study: Library Marketing Toolkit

The Library Marketing Toolkit (www.librarymarketingtoolkit.com/) was developed and is maintained by Ned Potter, an academic librarian who is the author of a book with the same title (Potter, 2012). This is an excellent site and includes access to a blog and information on essential tools and resources, and case studies. It is complemented by Potter's generic website (www.ned-potter.com/), which Potter maintains regularly. It is particularly useful for insights into the use of technology for marketing communications.

Summary

This chapter is concerned with the basic principles of designing and developing courses and other learning and teaching events. It covers the following topics: thinking about participants, basic design principles, levels of learning, basic design structure, design of individual learning activities, finding and using learning resources, reviewing the programme design, and marketing and promotion, which highlights the importance of a range of e-tools in the communication process as well as gaining the help and support of stakeholders. The next chapter considers design practice for face-to-face sessions, the flipped classroom, blended learning and online courses. Evaluation of the impact of learning and teaching interventions is discussed in Chapter 10.

References

ACRL (2014) *Framework for Information Literacy for Higher Education*, http://acrl.ala.org/ilstandards/?page_id=133.

Biggs, J. B. (2011) *Teaching for Quality Learning at University: what the student does*, McGraw-Hill Education (UK).

Bloom, B. S. (1956) *Taxonomy of Educational Objectives, Handbook 1: the cognitive domain*, David McKay Co. Inc.

Carncross, M. (2015) Redeveloping a Course with the Framework for Information Literacy for Higher Education from Skills to Process, *College and Research Libraries News*, **76** (5), 248–73.

Clow, K. E. and Baack, D. (2007) *Integrated Advertising, Promotion and Marketing Communications*, 3rd edn, Pearson Education.

McCarthy, B. and McCarthy, D. (2005) *Teaching Around the 4MAT®Cycle: designing instruction for diverse learners with diverse learning styles*, Corwin Press.

Potter, N. (2012) *The Library Marketing Toolkit*, Facet Publishing.

8

Designing face-to-face, blended and online courses

Introduction

In this chapter, the underlying principles of the design process which were considered in Chapter 7 are applied to a number of different learning and teaching situations – face-to-face learning, flipped classrooms, blended learning and online learning. As a reminder, these are the basic ideas that inform the programme or course design and development process:

- identification of aim or purpose, learning outcome(s) and required level of learning, e.g. using Bloom's taxonomy
- design of structure
- identification and use of learning resources
- design of learning and teaching activities
- design of assessment methods (formative or summative)
- pilot of the new programme.

Selected learning and teaching activities, described in Chapter 6, may be used within the course structure to enable students to achieve their learning outcomes.

Traditionally, programmes are designed on the assumption that students will work through them in a linear manner and this chapter provides guidance on typical structures for short courses (lasting for 15 minutes or more) or longer courses, e.g. one or two day events, which are delivered 100% face to face. The development of blended learning and online programmes enables individual learners to follow their own route through a series of learning and teaching activities. Consequently, their development and implementation is more complex.

Designing face-to-face sessions

The 4MAT approach described in Chapter 7 may be applied to workshops and teaching sessions which may last from half an hour through to a five-day intensive course. Figure 8.1 presents an overview structure for learning and teaching events; as explained in Chapter 7 the same structure is applied to individual learning and teaching activities. Thus students can go through the 4MAT cycle a number of times on the same course. One of the advantages of maintaining the same inner structure to a course and individual activities is that students soon learn it and it helps to guide them through their learning process.

Structure	Content
Introductions	Introductions – people, housekeeping, session
WHY Benefits of attending the session	Answers the questions: what will I learn in this session? What are the benefits to me of learning this subject or skill?
What Introduction to the main topic	Provides an outline of the main topic Formative assessment
How Practical activity	Hands-on activity, group activity, individual activity (as appropriate) Formative assessment
What if Any questions	Time for questions and answers
Summary and/or conclusion	Identify 3-5 main learning points from the session
Close session	Thank you, contact details, goodbyes

Figure 8.1 *General structure for a learning and teaching event*

Example: Introduction to referencing

This example session plan presented in Figure 8.2 opposite demonstrates my application of the 4MAT design method to a one-hour lecture on referencing which I delivered to 500 students.

Case study: The ANCIL lesson plan

There are many approaches to planning learning and teaching sessions, and in the example given above I used my preferred method. The development of new approaches to information literacy (see Chapter 3) has resulted in fresh interest in session plans. Secker and Coonan (2013) use the following headings in their indicative lesson plan:

COURSE TITLE

Purpose: what study or research need will be met?

Target audience

Learning outcome(s): what will participants know or be able to do by the end of the session?

ANCIL learning bands

    Practical skill

    Subject content

    Advanced information handling

    Learning to learn

Practicalities

    Format and duration of each session

Venue layout

    Equipment needed

Content

    Materials

    Activities and reflective components

Assessment and feedback mechanism

The institutional picture

    Which ANCIL strands are represented in the session content?

Where does this session dovetail or overlap with other provision in the institution?

Title: How to help yourself gain good grades in your assessed work			
Aim or purpose: To demonstrate the importance of using standard referencing techniques			
Learning outcome(s) By the end of the lecture, students will be able to: • explain the importance of using the Harvard method in their assessed work • understand the basic concepts of referencing • know how to find additional information and help.			
Resources required: PPT access to Blackboard			
4MAT approach	**Topic**	**Tutor activity**	**Student activity**
Introduction	Introduce self and topic Videoclip – 2 mins – previous year's student talking about his experiences	Speak Watch clip	Listen Watch clip
Why	Explain: benefits of accurate referencing – link to assessed work and marks; present statistics on student use of unfair means and the consequences	Speak	Listen
What including formative assessment	Use a visual metaphor to explain concept Students engage with activity through show of hands Provide a simple example and highlight key features	Explain metaphor using PowerPoint Explain using PowerPoint and images	Listen and engage with whole group activity Watch and listen
How including formative assessment	True and false quiz	Work through quiz	Students work in twos and threes

Figure 8.2 *Example lesson plan for a lecture on referencing (continued over)*

4MAT approach	Topic	Tutor activity	Student activity
What if	Explain links to assessed work Different kinds of sources How to find help on the library website Any other questions	Present a series of questions on PowerPoint Ask if there are any other questions	Answer questions as whole group Opportunity to ask questions
Close activity	Show Blackboard site with all resources Explain support from library and that you will send them all an e-mail with a LibGuide link Thank partipants, wish them well in their first assignment and say goodbye	Speaking with PowerPoint	Listen

Figure 8.2 *Continued*

Designing flipped classroom sessions

The 'flipped classroom' is a pedagogic model (Lakmal and Dawson, 2015), which reverses conventional approaches to teaching and learning. Traditionally face-to-face classroom time is spent by a tutor explaining or presenting new ideas, and this may be followed by some activities. In a flipped classroom, students explore the material outside the classroom and then spend time with the tutor clarifying and developing deeper knowledge through discussion and activities.

The use of flipped classrooms is often associated with technology and a range of media – video, audio or text-based – may be used to present the basic concepts to students. Diagnostic activities such as online self-assessment tests may be used to help motivate students and help them focus their out-of-class activities. The value of the flipped classroom approach is that the time spent in the classroom is focused on helping students to deepen their understanding and learning, rather than presenting basic information and ideas. The challenge is to ensure that students carry out the learning activity outside the classroom so they are well prepared for their learning experiences with their tutor.

The same design principles apply when designing flipped classroom courses or sessions as when designing more traditional training sessions: have a clear overall aim or purpose, and a set of specific learning objectives. The structure can be similar to that presented earlier in this chapter and involves using the 4MAT approach, but the learning and teaching activity should be organized into pre-classroom activities and classroom-based activities, as shown in Figure 8.3 on the opposite page.

Case study: A flipped classroom

Datig and Ruswig (2013) present their experiences of using a flipped classroom and describe their motivation as a result of wanting to develop active learning in the classroom, to avoid 'lecture fatigue', and to make better use of the prepared tutorials and guides that were already available in their library service. Their flipped classroom activities were based around four taught sessions on:

- searching databases
- keyword searching
- website evaluation
- identifying source types.

Students were provided with pre-session activities such as watching a video or reading a guide. Classroom time was focused on student activity and engagement, and example activities included group work, student presentations, class votes and hands-on tasks. The feedback from students and academics was positive. One of the challenges faced by the librarians was the distribution of pre-instruction session materials to the students before the class.

Structure	Content	Learning or teaching activity
Introductions	Introductions – people, housekeeping, session	Introductory video clip and e-mail
Why Benefits of attending the session	Answers the questions: what will I learn in this session? What are the benefits to me of learning this subject or skill?	Introductory video clip and e-mail
What Introduction to the main topic	Provide an outline of the main topic	Video clip or PowerPoint Formative assessment, e.g. quiz
How Practical activity	Hands-on activity, group activity, individual activity (as appropriate)	Face-to-face session involving learning activities Formative assessment, e.g. worksheet
What if Any questions	Time for questions and answers	Face-to-face session involving learning activities
Summary and/or conclusion	Identify 3–5 main learning points from the session	Face-to-face session plus follow-up summary via e-mail and/or video clip
Close session	Thank you, contact details, goodbyes	Either in the face-to-face session and/or via e-mail

Figure 8.3 *Example of the design of a flipped classroom session*

Designing blended learning courses

Blended learning involves a combination of face-to-face and online learning activities, and it is becoming increasingly common within higher education, where the learning platform is often the organization's virtual learning environment.

Reasons for developing and delivering blended learning training programmes include:

- making learning more accessible, engaging and relevant
- providing more flexible learning opportunities
- reducing the amount of time spent on face-to-face learning activities by shifting the balance to more online learning activities

- integrating practitioner-based experiences with classroom-based learning
- exploiting ICT and training facilities
- demonstrating the use of leading edge technologies
- meeting student expectations.

Blended learning programmes may include:

- a rich mixture of face-to-face and/or online learning activities
- use of different media including text, audio or visual media
- opportunities to give learners choices, e.g. of learning methods and/or activities
- alternative approaches to contacting and working with each other including face-to-face sessions, e-mail and message systems, phone, Skype and online discussion groups.

The balance of methods will depend on the aims and learning outcomes, the participants and their context, and the trainer. Figure 8.4 shows an overview of the continuum of online to face-to-face learning with blended learning taking place in the middle ground.

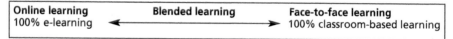

Figure 8.4 *Overview of the continuum of online to face-to-face learning*

Commonly used online learning and teaching tools include:

- e-mails
- video clips and podcasts
- diagnostic tests and quizzes
- online assessment methods
- guides and handbooks
- social networking tools, e.g. Twitter, Instagram, Flickr and Pinterest
- blogs and wikis
- online communication tools, e.g. discussion groups, chat and messaging
- online face-to-face communications, e.g. Skype and FaceTime.

Blended learning offers flexibility of time and space to learners and tutors. For example, the time involved in physically attending a course may be reduced through the use of e-learning activities. Individuals may choose when they engage with their e-learning and select from a menu of opportunities to create an individualized learning experience that meets their needs and interests.

The same design principles that are used for face-to-face programmes are relevant to blended learning, including the identification of an aim or aims and learning outcomes. The programme designed needs to ensure that the four elements introduced in the 4MAT approach are covered in the blended learning programme:

- **why** the participant needs to achieve the learning outcomes: why they will benefit from engaging in the training event
- **what** the participant will learn: the basic ideas or content
- **how** the material covered in the training event applies to practice
- the opportunity to ask '**what if**' questions, which are often used as an opportunity for participants to relate their learning to their own particular situation, e.g. an assessment activity.

The following case study indicates how blended learning may be used to deliver a course on referencing skills.

Case study: Use of blended learning when delivering a course on referencing skills

Table 8.1 provides a breakdown of the structure, content and learning activities for a blended learning course.

There are many different approaches to structuring blended learning programmes and courses, and Table 8.2 shows some common structures:

Table 8.1 *Breakdown of the structure, content and learning activity of a blended learning course*

Structure	Content	Learning activity
Introduction and welcome	Introduction and welcome	Read e-mail
Why Benefits of engaging with course	Learning outcomes Benefits: good marks and avoidance of accusations of plagiarism Demonstrate appropriate academic practices	Watch video clip – tutor plus student
What Covers basic ideas of how to reference Formative assessment	Introduction to basic referencing skills	Watch PowerPoint Complete an online quiz
How Formative test on understanding of basic rules Apply rules to own assignment	Basic rules In classroom, students bring their draft reference list for their first assignment	Online quiz Classroom activity Input and support from tutor Informal assessment and feedback from peers and tutor
What if	Content generated by student questions	Classroom activity Students ask questions and clarify any uncertainties about referencing
Close	Summary; information on additional help and support	Take note of further information and support

Table 8.2 *Common structures of blended learning courses and programmes*

Time	Wrap-around face-to-face core	Wrap around online learning core	Flipped classroom approach	Integrated approach
	Online learning activities	Face-to-face activities	Online learning activities	Online and face-to-face approach
	Face-to-face activities	Online learning activities	Face-to-face activities	Online and face-to-face approach
	Online learning activities	Face-to-face activities	Face-to-face activities	Online and face-to-face approach

- wrap-around face-to-face core
- wrap-around online learning core
- the flipped classroom approach
- the integrated approach.

The previous case study uses a flipped classroom approach with much of the content being delivered through online learning activities. The face-to-face session is used to put the ideas into practice and provide opportunities for questioning and discussion.

Case study: Developing a blended learning course for research students

Coombs (2015) described an initiative, which started off with the aim of converting a face-to-face literature searching course aimed at research students to an online course. Feedback from students suggested that they liked the face-to-face course because it provided opportunities for them to meet and network with other research students, and they could practise their online searches with a librarian available to give them help and advice. Based on this feedback, the researchers decided not to develop an online course but a blended learning one.

The first three units are online: an introduction to literature searching and how it fits into the literature review, how to identify key words, and how to identify appropriate sources. Students can work through these online courses at their own pace and when it suits them. At the ends of these three units, students are asked to produce a reflective summary, which is then uploaded into their virtual learning environment (Blackboard) and the librarians provide feedback on this summary via e-mail. Later students can choose to attend a face-to-face session on advance searching and current awareness.

Coombs (2015) concludes by suggesting that the blended approach appears to meet the needs of the diverse group of PhD students. The obstacles experienced included technology, getting the tone right in the online learning materials, and the difficulty of re-creating a peer support community in the online elements (as compared with a 100% face-to-face course). The benefits of the blended approach were that it helped to bring all students up to a basic level before they went on to more advanced searching; it permitted peer-to-peer support and community building; it provided distance students and campus-based students with access to the same information and support; and the use of the reflective piece of work helped the librarians to develop their understanding of the research being carried out within their discipline.

Design of online courses

The design principles for online courses are similar to those used when designing face-to-face or blended learning courses. The main difference is that a virtual learning environment or other online space gives students access to the whole learning process and associated resources. Therefore learning environment should ideally have the following characteristics:

- be visually attractive
- have clear and accessible text
- show clear navigation routes with options to move forward and backwards, and jump sections
- use a variety of media so that students use as many of their senses (visual, auditory and kinesthetic) as possible
- provide opportunities for assessment of learning
- provide opportunities for interaction and feedback
- be accessible to people with special needs (see chapter 2)
- be accessible on a wide range of technologies, e.g. laptops, tablets and smart phones.

The structure of an online course is likely to be similar to that of a face-to-face one and may involve the following elements:

- welcome and introduction, using techniques such as:
  — a video clip from librarian or information worker
  — a text-based welcome
- indication of the benefits of completing the online course, using techniques such as:
  — a video clip recommendation from tutor and/or student(s)
  — text-based recommendations from tutor and/or students(s)
  — a diagnostic test
- introduction to the topic, using techniques such as:
  — text
  — multimedia clips
  — additional resources and links
- learning activities such as:
  — worksheets
  — self-assessment tests
  — online or library-based activities
  — suggestions for other work
- assessment activities such as:
  — online tests
  — online activities

- question time through the use of:
  — frequently asked question documents
  — opportunities to contact a librarian, e.g. via e-mail, chat or text
- a summary, e.g. video clip, diagram or short piece of text
- close of tutorial through:
  — production of test results, certificate or digital badge
  — an evaluation activity
  — a thank you and goodbye statement.

Example: Online course on teaching large groups

Aim

To provide guidance to library staff who are involved in preparing and delivering sessions to large groups

Benefits

Working through this online learning resource will enable you to be prepared and confident about delivering to large groups.

Intended learning outcomes

As a result of working through this online course, individuals will be:

- prepared for teaching large groups
- able to use basic strategies to ensure their session is interesting and engaging
- able to develop a strategy for dealing with challenging situations.

Online course structure

See Figure 8.5 opposite for an overview of an online course structure.

Timing

It takes individual learners between 60 and 120 minutes to work through this online course.

Summary

This chapter provides an overview of designing courses, workshops and training sessions. The 4MAT approach to design is used as an underlying framework in this chapter and applied to face-to-face training events, the flipped classroom, blended learning and online learning. The case studies demonstrate how these ideas can be applied in practice.

Approximate time (mins)	Content	Media	Individual activities
5	Introduction	Text and video clip	Read and watch
5	Ask what is a large group?	Text	Read
5	Checking out the learning environment	Text	Read
15	Checklist of questions and actions before the session	Checklist	Complete checklist
15	Underlying pedagogy	Text plus video clip	Read, watch, complete questions
5	Preparing your session	Text	Read
10	Use of technology	PPT example - illustrating different technologies	Read and watch
10	Use of activities	Examples: quiz, mini case study, interview Followed by a quiz about use of activities	Read Complete quiz
10	Working with a colleague	Video clip	Watch
10	Contingency planning	Text Checklist	Read Complete quiz
10	Challenging situations	Text plus reflective activity 4 mini-case studies	Read Complete activity
5	Case study	Case study	Read and respond to questions
10	Personal reflection and action planning	Text plus activity	Read and complete action plan pro-forma
5	Summary and close	Video clip	

Figure 8.5 *Overview of an online course structure*

References

Coombs, J. (2015) Literature Searching for Research Students: meeting the needs of a diverse student population, *SCONUL Focus*, **64**, 63–4.

Datig, I. and Ruswick, C. (2013) Four Quick Flips: activities for the information literacy classroom, *College and Research Libraries News*, **74** (5), 249–57.

Lakmal, A. and Dawson, P. (2015) Motivation and Cognitive Load in the Flipped Classroom: definition, rationale and a call for research, *Higher Education Research & Development*, **34** (1), 1–14.

Secker, J. and Coonan, E. (eds) (2013) *Rethinking Information Literacy: a practical framework for supporting learning*, Facet Publishing.

9

Delivering learning experiences

Introduction

This chapter provides guidance on delivering learning experiences either face to face or online. It covers the following themes: preparing yourself, face-to-face delivery, online delivery and co-facilitation.

A useful structure for thinking about delivering learning experience is to consider the following aspects of the course or programme: preparing yourself, getting off to a good start, facilitating the learning processes, and closing the course. For both virtual and face-to-face courses think about individual learners, group dynamics and yourself. Many tutors find that they spend so much time focusing on individuals or the whole group that they forget about themselves. This is counter-productive as personal awareness may provide important indicators about the learning process and the experiences of learners.

Preparing yourself

Before you start delivering a course or programme, whether face to face or online, it is worth asking yourself a number of questions about the course, the students and yourself. The questions listed below will help to ensure that you have considered a range of factors which are likely to affect the success of the course.

Ask yourself these questions about the course:

- Am I confident about the course design?
- Have I piloted the course or, if this isn't possible, have I talked it through with a colleague and run through it in my mind?
- Am I familiar with the learning environment (virtual or physical)? If not what do I need to do to make myself confident in this environment? Do I have access to help, e.g. via phone or e-mail, and do I have the necessary contact details?
- Do I have all the relevant learning and teaching materials?

Ask yourself these questions about the students:

- Do I know who is likely to attend the event?
- Do any of the students require special facilities or adjustments to enable them to gain full benefit from the course? Have I made the necessary adjustments?
- How have they been informed about the event and what they will gain from it (the benefits)?
- Have they received the relevant information, e.g. location, timing and/or how to access the online site?
- Am I able to send a welcome e-mail to students?

Ask yourself these questions about yourself:

- Am I confident about all aspects of delivering the course?
- Do I need additional help or support: either before or during the course?
- Have I scheduled the necessary time into my diary so that I can attend to the students and course?
- Have I developed a contingency plan, e.g. for technology or other failures?
- Have I developed some additional activities as a contingency plan, e.g. if the timing doesn't go to plan?

Face-to-face delivery
Getting started
In colleges and universities, there is often little choice about the rooms that are allocated for teaching. If you are allocated a room that you have not used previously it is worth visiting it beforehand to check the facilities. In large learning spaces, e.g. lecture theatres, in addition to checking the technology and lighting arrangements, if you are teaching in a room that is new to you it is worthwhile going into it when it is empty and sitting in different seats, e.g. at the front, back and edges of the room, so that you gain a sense of what the students will see and how close or distant they may feel from the tutor.

Many universities and colleges use the holiday periods to upgrade their information systems. If you are one of the first people to be scheduled to teach in the room after a holiday period there may be some surprises, e.g. new kit, unfinished cabling, absent cables or connections. Check the facilities a day or two before you are due to use them. This double checking could help you avoid being in an embarrassing situation!

When you are scheduled to deliver a course, if possible arrive early. This gives you time to double check the room and facilities, including:

- the seating arrangements

- technology including testing use of video clips and other digital media
- access to a phone
- lighting
- the location of toilets
- emergency exits and arrangements.

Once you have carried out all the checks position yourself in the room so that you can meet and greet everyone as they arrive for their course. This gives you an opportunity to introduce yourself and perhaps get to know some people's names. It also gives them a chance to 'size you up' and begin to get to know you. Some people use music to produce a positive learning environment and switch it off as an indicator of the start of the session.

Act in a decisive manner once it is time to start the session. A typical start of a session will involve you doing the following:

- welcoming everyone to the event by greeting people and making eye contact; start off with positive phrases: 'welcome to this course; I am really pleased to be here and hope that we all have a very successful time together'
- starting enthusiastically and with energy, which helps to set the tone and pace for the training event
- getting people involved by using an ice breaker (see Chapter 6 and below) to help people settle down and relax into the session; the sooner individuals are engaged with a small group of colleagues the quicker they will relax and participate in whole group activities
- grabbing people's interest by using stories, appropriate humour, a video clip or a quick quiz to gain people's attention and interest in the session.

Delivering the course

There are different ways of involving everyone in the learning and teaching process, which should have been designed into the course at the course design stage. However, it is worth having some additional examples that may be used if your course is not going as planned, e.g. if students appear tired and need to be re-energized. Here are some ideas:

- Ask everyone to introduce themselves and say what they want to gain from the session. Write this up on a flipchart or whiteboard. At the end of the session, refer back to this information and check that everyone has achieved their aims.
- Use an introductory activity (an ice breaker).
- Use people's names throughout the session.
- Refer to comments that students have made earlier in the session.

- Show your interest and enthusiasm through your verbal and body language.
- Treat everyone with respect.
- Be culturally sensitive.
- If anyone has additional needs double check that you have made appropriate adjustments for them.
- Ask people to work in different groups, e.g. pairs, trios and quads.
- Have breaks and give people the opportunity to go outside for a few minutes.
- Use real life stories.
- Use different activities, which engage different senses, e.g. sight, sound and touch.
- Use games.
- Use rewards, e.g. sweets, fresh fruit or small items of stationery.
- Ensure that everyone feels noticed and cared-for.
- Give lots of praise and encouragement.

Timing issues sometimes arise in courses and teaching sessions. Starting late makes the session get off to a bad start, which may make it difficult to manage the timing for the whole event. Sometimes it is impossible to start on time, e.g. half the group may be late due to problems with an over-running previous session or issues with public transport. In this case, it is worth explaining the situation to the group and making a clear decision about when you will start: 'Thank you for being here on time. It is now time to start but half the group is late. We will give them an additional 10 minutes and then we will start.'

Another issue relates to starting too slowly. If you get off to a slow start, e.g. your introductions lack energy, or administrative activities take longer than required, it can be difficult to re-energize the group. Sometimes introducing an additional game or stand-up activity helps to regain control over the pace of the event.

Facilitating the learning process
When you are facilitating a course it is important that you help to ensure that your students achieve their learning outcomes. One approach to this is to monitor:

- progress through the course
- individual students
- the group
- yourself
- the physical environment.

Monitoring progress throughout the course involves keeping an eye on your course plan and the timing. Are you covering the material and the activities as intended? Do you need to cut out some materials or activities? Do you need to introduce some extra activities or information?

Observe individual students and notice whether or not they are engaged in the course. It is advisable to observe their body language and look in particular for signs of interest, attentiveness, engagement, boredom, stress or anxiety. Notice if anyone looks disgruntled or dissatisfied. I also notice whether or not they are working positively with their peers. Sometimes, there are predictable reasons for individual behaviour, e.g. at the beginning of the academic year it is not unusual for one or more international students to be jet-lagged and this affects their ability to learn. Once you have identified students with an issue decide whether or not to intervene; if you decide to intervene think about whether to do so directly or indirectly. In general, it is advisable to deal with individual issues privately, e.g. in a break or during an activity.

It is also important to monitor the whole group; notice their energy levels and whether or not they are engaged in the learning and teaching activities. If their energy is low think about how to create more energy and enthusiasm, e.g. through physical movement (even changing seats introduces a new dynamic), introducing a different activity or having an extra break. If the energy is too high and the group appears to be over-excited it is worthwhile slowing down the pace by using your voice and body language, and/or introducing an individual activity or challenge.

Sometimes, issues such as a fire alarm or serious illness cause a disruption to the course. Once the disruption has ended assess whether or not there is sufficient time to resume the training session. If it is resumed give everyone a few minutes to settle down and make a clear statement about moving on and focusing on the course. You may find that you need to change your course plan to fit the remaining time. If it is impossible to resume the session send everyone an e-mail with an appropriate message and advice on what to do next.

I always monitor myself when I am delivering courses and other learning and teaching events. I notice whether or not I am feeling comfortable with the course delivery and, in particular, with the individual students and the whole group. If I am feeling over-excited and 'hyper' then perhaps I am causing this reaction in the students or perhaps I am responding to them. If I am feeling bored perhaps I am delivering something that bores me and, if this is the case, then I will certainly be delivering a boring session and so will need to change it. Quickly!

Finally, monitor the physical environment. What is the temperature? Is it too hot, cold or just right? Is there external noise that is disrupting the course? Are there flickering lights or is the lighting too strong or too weak? These and other physical factors may all adversely affect the course. If it is possible to manage the physical environment then do either adjust the thermostat yourself or call the estate's staff. It is sometimes impossible to change the physical environment and, in this case, it is sometimes best to acknowledge it and apologize for any discomfort caused by it.

The basic message in this section is that when you are delivering your course you should constantly monitor the course itself, the students, yourself and the physical environment. Decide whether or not to intervene if you identify any issues. In general, being open and honest and presenting information in a constructive manner tends to work well with course participants.

Closing the course

Finally, remember to close the session:

- Ensure 'loose ends' are completed.
- Provide a brief summary or ask the students to summarize their learning.
- Encourage (structured) reflection and evaluation on group process.
- Highlight group achievements.
- Thank the students for their contributions and work.
- Formally close the course.

Case study: Eight tips from the trenches

Scripps-Hoekstra (2013) was a high school teacher before becoming a librarian and she has written some valuable advice on how this experience helps to inform her approach to teaching information literacy. These are her eight tips for teaching:

1. Welcome your students: greet the students as they enter the room.
2. Work the room: move around the room and make full use of all the physical space.
3. Bring it to their level: move physically so that you are not talking down to students but working at eye level.
4. Make it mandatory: use language that is directive rather than suggestive. Instead of 'I'd like you to do Y' say 'Now will you go to X and do Y.' Make sure that this is followed up by a simple 'please' and 'thank you'.
5. See, hear and write: use visual and auditory learning methods; encourage students to make notes.
6. Try something new: experiment, use new ideas and take (calculated) risks.
7. Communicate enthusiasm.
8. Objectives matter: use learning objectives (or outcomes) as a means of helping to focus your work and its impact.

She writes

The process of becoming an excellent teacher requires years of hard work, thoughtful innovation, and continual reflection. Effective teachers have a strong foundation in educational theory coupled with an understanding that often the smaller details and interactions can make a good lesson great. While this level of mastery will take time, remember that you are not alone on this journey. No matter your instructional

background or experience, by collaborating with colleagues to share effective
strategies and helpful tips, we can all help each other along the way.

(Scripps-Hoekstra, 2013, 253)

Online delivery

Delivering an online course or a blended learning course requires a slightly different range of communication and learning and teaching skills to those required for delivering purely face-to-face courses. However, it involves a similar approach to that described in the previous section on face-to-face delivery, which demonstrated that you need to get started, facilitate the learning process and close the course.

Getting started

Getting started delivering an online course or activity involves making sure that you:

- prepare your virtual learning environment, including:
  — a welcome message
  — some information about yourself including your availability online
  — a photograph uploaded online (optional)
  — clear guidance about the course or activity
  — well labelled and organized resources
- ensure that everyone receives instructions on how to log in to the system or the space reserved for that course
- welcome everyone (including late-comers) to the online course or activity
- grab students' interest; don't over use text and use a range of media to engage students
- involve students in the learning process, e.g. use a simple activity such as giving brief introductions, or ask them to post up their photo
- provide a structure for getting started, e.g. agreement of group rules such as levels and timing of interactions.

Facilitating the online learning process

If you are leading an online course where individuals are working through a programme by themselves, you may want to check whether or not they have logged into the system and are working through it. The system's analytics will be useful here. If you notice that individuals have dropped out or that they have not been online for some time decide whether or not to intervene.

When you are leading online courses that include group work it is important that you monitor:

- progress through the course or online activity

- individual students
- the group.

To monitor progress throughout the course keep an eye on your course plan and the timing. Are the students working through the material and activities as intended? Do you need to provide some additional clarification or guidance, to cut out some materials or activities, or to introduce some extra activities or information?

Monitor the online behaviour of individual students and encourage their participation. Acknowledge individual responses and efforts, and use them as an opportunity to open discussions and involve others. Sometimes it is appropriate to ask for volunteers or to allocate online roles to individual members, e.g. to give a summary of a particular thread of discussion or of an article. If you observe that someone is not engaging with an online activity you could send them a private e-mail to ask if they require additional help or support.

Monitoring the whole group requires thinking about the dynamics and asking yourself questions such as:

- Is anyone dominating the group?
- Are members being included or excluded?
- Are group expectations about individual response times appropriate? If not, consider whether or not you need to intervene.
- Is the online activity taking place at an appropriate pace? If it appears too fast or slow then should you intervene?
- Is the language inclusive and respectful?

If you are leading a very lively online group with lots of activity it is helpful to ensure that summaries of main points and activities are posted online regularly. It helps everyone to know the main themes and issues that are being explored. You could do this yourself or ask one of the students to take on this activity.

It is also worthwhile reflecting and observing your own online behaviour by asking yourself questions such as:

- How often are you visible online? Is this level of visibility appropriate?
- Are you giving individuals and the group sufficient time to do the work themselves?
- Are you playing 'ping pong' with individual group members and so excluding some people?
- Are you using open questions as a means of facilitating learning?
- If individuals break the agreed ground rules do you address the issue (either privately or through the discussion group)?
- Do you encourage quieter group members to join in?

- Is your use of language, e.g. grammar and spelling, correct?

Closing the course or activity
At this stage, it is likely that you will need to:

- ensure 'loose ends' are completed
- provide a brief summary or ask students to summarize their learning
- encourage (structured) reflection and evaluation on group process
- highlight group achievements
- thank group members for their contributions and work
- formally close the course or activity.

Sometimes group members want to continue working together in a virtual setting and establish a group on social media such as LinkedIn or Facebook. If you are invited to join the group make a professional decision about whether or not you make the commitment.

Co-facilitation
Library and information workers frequently work with other professional groups, e.g. research scientists, academics and IT trainers, and co-facilitate the design and delivery of courses or learning experiences. There are different forms of co-facilitation ranging from simply sharing the delivery of a training session to becoming embedded in a team.

Co-facilitation involves two or more people sharing the delivery. These are some common approaches:

- taking turns to deliver different parts of the course
- taking different roles, e.g. one person is the main presenter while the second person works the technology
- sharing everything 100%.

The main advantage of sharing the delivery of the session is that you have someone to support you and are able to provide greater variety to your course students. If you are working with a colleague in this way it is sensible to spend time together beforehand planning the session and working out how you will co-deliver it. In particular, it is worth thinking through how you would deal with a situation where there is some disagreement between you.

The term 'embedded librarian' is used to describe the situation where a library or information worker works in a setting (physical or virtual) that enables close collaboration with another professional team or group. Embedded librarianship commonly takes place in academic contexts where the librarian works as part of an academic team delivering a course to a group of students. Kumar, Wu and

Reynolds (2014) write about the evaluation of the experience and impact of an embedded librarian in a health sciences course. Their research noted that the role of the librarian had changed from responding to reference enquiries to becoming an active part of the teaching team. This shift in role was supported through a staff development process, which included learning about the discipline and the actual course including its assessment, and developing online facilitation skills. The students' research skills improved as a result of the embedded librarian being involved in the course.

Hardenbrook (2013) provides advice on how to get started as an embedded librarian. To get started:

- Identify a library friendly colleague who is likely to be receptive to the idea.
- Target appropriate courses or modules, e.g. those with a research component such as projects or dissertations.
- Contact the colleague and ask for his or her support. Provide information about the idea of an embedded librarian and the benefits it is likely to bring the students.
- Once agreement has been reached to work together spend some time working through how you will work together in partnership.
- Ensure that you have access to the relevant course or module on the virtual learning environment.

To work as part of the team:

- If there is an introductory face-to-face session make sure that you are there and visible as part of the team.
- Post an online introduction with photograph. This could be a video. Make it clear what you are there to do. Let the students know how often you will be online.
- Engage in appropriate discussion fora and, if appropriate, create your own discussion forum.
- Introduce relevant learning resources.

To encourage students to ask questions:

- Be welcoming. Encourage questions. If the discussion forum is quiet then perhaps introduce a posting that talks about a common issue students may experience and give them guidance on resolving it.
- Develop a list of 'ready to go' questions. These can be introduced into the discussion at regular times, e.g. weekly, to encourage engagement.
- If a student e-mails you privately with a question tell them you will answer it in the discussion forum. Remember to maintain their anonymity.

- Post information and guidance using different media: print, video, images.

What next?

- You may want to develop your practice further, e.g. by becoming embedded in more modules or courses.
- Develop some higher-level activities that can be embedded into the course, e.g. self-paced tutorials, quizzes or interviews with students.
- Evaluate the experience. Find out the impact you are having on students' progress.
- Write up your experience and encourage colleagues to get involved.

Summary
This chapter focuses on delivering learning experiences either face to face or online. It provides a structure for delivering any kind of learning or teaching event: preparing for the event or course, getting off to a good start, facilitating the learning processes, and ending the event or course. Library and information workers who deliver virtual and/or face-to-face courses need to monitor individual learners and the whole group, as well as themselves. This enables the session plan to be adapted flexibly to ensure that the students achieve their learning outcomes.

References
Hardenbrook, J. (2013) *Embedded Librarian 101: how to get started*, https://mrlibrarydude.wordpress.com/2013/06/17/embedded-librarian-101-how-to-get-started.

Kumar, S., Wu, L. and Reynolds, R. (2014) Embedded Librarian within an Online Health Informatics Graduate Research Course: a case study, *Medical Reference Services Quarterly*, **33** (1), 51–9.

Scripps-Hoekstra, L. (2013) Eight Tips from the Trenches: how experience teaching high school informs my approach to information literacy instruction, *College and Research Libraries News*, **74** (5), 252–3.

10

Evaluation of learning and teaching activities and courses

Introduction

In many countries student experience and satisfaction are high on the agenda of universities and colleges, and students are regularly asked for their feedback on all aspects of their academic life. The results of this feedback are used to inform change and improvements, and as performance measures within institutions; summarized results may be displayed in league tables.

The provision of library and information services to students is regularly monitored through a range of quality assurance and enhancement processes. Library and information workers who are module leaders or tutors on credit-bearing modules are likely to be involved in specific course-related quality assurance and enhancement processes, such as annual monitoring, so it is important for them to understand their institutional policy and practices.

In contrast, some of the activities of library and information workers, e.g. workshops, online courses, giving one-to-one support, may not be explicitly included in the institutional quality assurance and enhancement processes that monitor courses and modules. It is therefore important for library and information service staff to think about how they wish to evaluate those of their activities that directly support student learning and to have appropriate systems in place.

Different countries have their own systems of quality control and enhancement and this chapter provides a brief overview of these processes in the UK. Many of the underlying principles are the same in higher education in other countries, although their organization may be based on factors such as geography, type of institution and type of course, and the evaluation may be led by government or other agencies.

The main part of this chapter is concerned with the evaluation of the impact of learning and teaching activities, e.g. short courses, online courses, and blended learning courses. It starts with a summary of some of the research findings of Schilling and Applegate (2012), which gives an insight into important distinctions when measuring students' attitudes, learning or behaviour. The next section looks at practical approaches to evaluating the impact of learning and teaching activities and covers a wide range of methods, from student assignments through to tests, and gives case studies that demonstrate the value of using a number of tools together when evaluating these interventions.

UK quality control and enhancement processes

In the UK, the Quality Assurance Agency (QAA; www.qaa.ac.uk/) safeguards standards and works to improve the quality of higher education in colleges and universities including UK provision overseas. It is helpful to understand the language of quality assurance. Here are some common terms:

- academic standards: the level of achievement that a student has to reach in order to gain a particular academic award
- academic quality: the provision of appropriate and effective learning, teaching and assessment opportunities to enable students to achieve their award
- quality assurance: 'the systematic monitoring and evaluation of learning and teaching, and the processes that support them, to make sure that the standards of academic awards meet UK expectations, and that the quality of the student learning experience is being safeguarded and improved' (QAA)
- quality enhancement: 'the process by which higher education providers systematically improve the quality of provision and the ways in which student learning is supported' (QAA)
- learning opportunities: 'the provision made for students' learning, including planned programmes of study, teaching, assessment, academic and personal support, resources (such as libraries and information systems, laboratories or studios) and staff development' (QAA).

A key document is the *UK Quality Code for Higher Education* (the Quality Code), which provides a reference point for determining how higher education institutions set, describe and assure the academic standards of their awards and programmes, and the quality of their learning opportunities. The purpose of the Quality Code is to:

- safeguard the academic standards of UK higher education
- assure the quality of the learning opportunities that UK higher education offers to students
- promote continuous and systematic improvement in UK higher education
- ensure that information about UK higher education is publicly available.

(QAA, 2014a)

The Quality Code is divided into an introduction and three main parts that cover the areas of focus for quality assurance and enhancement. Note that the use of external examiners is unique to the UK system. The structure of the Quality Code is presented in Table 10.1.

Table 10.1 *The structure of the Quality Code (QAA 2014a)*

Structure	Detailed content
General introduction	
Part A: Setting and maintaining academic standards	Qualifications frameworks Characteristics statements Credit frameworks Subject benchmark statements
Part B: Assuring and Enhancing Academic Quality	Chapter B1: Programme Design, Development and Approval This Chapter addresses the initial design and development of a programme and the processes which lead to a decision by the degree-awarding body that it may be delivered in the agreed form. Chapter B2: Recruitment, Selection and Admission to Higher Education This Chapter focuses on the interconnected policies and procedures related to the recruitment, selection and admission of students to higher education. It offers a framework for assuring quality, and provides guidance to higher education providers and those involved in recruitment, selection and admission. Chapter B3: Learning and Teaching This Chapter focuses on the learning opportunities that higher education providers make available to students and on the staff who teach and who support learning, including those staff who are not employees of the higher education provider and/or are not based at the provider. Chapter B4: Enabling Student Development and Achievement This Chapter addresses the ways in which higher education providers enable students to develop and achieve their academic, personal and professional potential. Chapter B5: Student Engagement This Chapter covers student engagement at undergraduate and postgraduate level, irrespective of location, mode of study, teaching delivery, or discipline. The Chapter focuses on the provision of an inclusive environment for student engagement. Chapter B6: Assessment of Students and the Recognition of Prior Learning This Chapter deals with the assessment of student learning, both learning which is achieved as part of a defined programme offered by a higher education provider, and learning at the equivalent level achieved outside the defined programme of study. The Chapter covers all forms of assessment used in the context of taught provision, and for the recognition of prior learning. Chapter B7: External Examining This Chapter is designed to ensure that external examining can operate in a way which is transparent, rigorous, and as consistent as possible across all UK higher education institutions, taking into account institutions' autonomy and differences in their mission, size, organizational structures and range of provision. Chapter B8: Programme Monitoring and Review This Chapter discusses the mechanisms which higher education providers use to reflect on a programme once it is running, and to determine how it can be improved. This Chapter also addresses matters relating to closure of existing programmes. Chapter B9: Academic Appeals and Student Complaints This Chapter sets out principles for addressing academic appeals and complaints about the quality of learning opportunities by students in higher education providers.

(Continued over)

Table 10.1 *Continued*	
	Chapter B10: Managing Higher Education Provision with Others This Chapter is based on the key principle that the delivery of learning opportunities with others, wherever and however organized, should widen learning opportunities without prejudice either to the academic standard of the award or the quality of what is offered to students. Chapter B11: Research Degrees
Part C: Information about Higher Education Provision	This single chapter sets out an expectation concerning the provision of valid, reliable, useful and accessible information by HEIs for the public.

In addition to its role in promoting quality and standards, the QAA supports higher education institutions in enhancing the quality of education through sharing good practice and ideas via publications, research and events. An example of one of their reports is *What Students Think of their Higher Education* (QAA, 2014b). It includes students' comments about their experiences of library and information services.

In the UK, individual universities and colleges define their quality assurance and enhancement processes, which are underpinned by the QAA's Quality Code. Typically, they consist of a number of elements:

- approval of new courses and awards
- annual review of courses and modules
- periodic review
- external examiners
- student feedback.

Each higher education institution has a quality and standards (or equivalent) office, which manages the academic framework and has an annual cycle of activity culminating in a series of formal reports. Formal committees, such as a quality committee, are responsible for ensuring the quality of all modules and courses, and report to the premier academic committee, e.g. Academic Council, annually.

Library and information workers who are responsible for credit-bearing modules or who contribute to these modules are involved in the annual review of courses and modules. Therefore students on their modules undergo an annual review process by completing module evaluation forms, and attendance at course committees and related activities and events. This provides valuable feedback on the module and students' responses to it.

Research on evaluation of learning and teaching in academic libraries

In a journal article, Schilling and Applegate, who are based in the USA, give a useful critical review of approaches to evaluating the quality and impact of library learning and teaching activities (Schilling and Applegate, 2012). They highlight the importance of library and information services using a systematic process for evaluating the educational impact of work, which is likely to involve a combination of quantitative and qualitative methods. Schilling and Applegate identify a number of key questions:

- What evaluation measures are commonly used for evaluating library instruction?
- What are the pros and cons of popular evaluation measures?
- What are the relationships between measures of skills versus measures of attitudes and behaviour?

They identified different approaches to measuring the impact of learning and teaching activities including:

- student attitudes: surveys
- evidence of student learning: practical exercises, assignments, e.g. essays, reports, projects, written knowledge, tests, portfolios, products, journals and logs
- student behaviour: library usage.

Schilling and Applegate (2012) emphasize that the timing of evaluation is important and discuss formative and summative evaluation. Formative evaluation is concerned with tracking student progress during the learning process; summative evaluation takes place at a fixed point either at the end of the learning and teaching process, or in the future. Summative evaluation was the most commonly used approach Schilling and Applegate found in their research and they identified some of the issues related to this form of evaluation, including low response rates in surveys, inability to control for a variety of variables, and the challenge of not having access to individual learners and the products of their learning activities (Schilling and Applegate, 2012).

Table 10.2, on the next page, provides a summary of measures of performance and the advantages and disadvantages of each method.

By using a combination of methods, e.g. performance measures, attitude measures and counts of library and resource usage, data can be correlated so that the educational impact of courses may be determined. However, this is a time consuming process and if only a segment of the student population is taking part in library and information service learning opportunities then it is extremely difficult to track a relatively small number of students and the educational impact of these interventions.

Table 10.2 *The advantages and disadvantages of various measures of performance*

	Advantages	Disadvantages
Example performance measures (knowledge and skills) Tests, course products, projects, portfolios, research papers, essays, posters, literature reviews, dissertation	Product produced as part of course rather than a separate activity for library staff	Levels of co-ordination and access required with academic staff Products may not provide the best evidence for assessing learning from the information or digital literacy course or learning activity Variables such as affect, values, perceptions and beliefs are not necessarily represented in the product
Example measures of attitude (e.g. satisfaction, confidence, comfort, likes, dislikes, preferences, interests etc) Surveys, questionnaires	Relatively simple and easy to implement	They are not useful in determining student learning, e.g. students may be over-confident and over-rate their knowledge and skills
Library and resource usage Use of business analytics Self-reported surveys	System analytics provide hard data about actual usage; they are relatively easy to capture and analyse Self-reported surveys also enable libraries to capture information about student attitudes and perceptions	Analytics do not provide information about attitudes and perceptions of users Self-reported surveys may not be accurate; there may be low response rates

Schilling and Applegate (2012, 266) observed the following:

- Practical exercises were the most efficacious way to document actual applied, practical skills.
- Written tests were not the equivalent of a practical searching exercise in terms of measuring applied, practical skills.
- Students were poor self-judges of their own skill levels. In fact, their attitudes evidenced the 'satisfied but inept' phenomena.
- Students were excellent self-judges of their attitudes, feelings, beliefs and perceptions.
- Certain attitudes went hand-in-hand, like confidence and satisfaction or frustration and dissatisfaction.
- Attitudes, feelings, beliefs and perceptions were not indicative of actual knowledge and learning.

Evaluation in practice

This section is concerned with practical approaches to evaluation. The evaluation process starts at the design stage of the learning and teaching activity when decisions need to be made about how it will be evaluated. The purpose of evaluation is to answer questions aimed at different audiences.

These are questions to ask the library and information service as a whole:

- To what extent did the learning and teaching activities support our goals and objectives, and key performance indicators?
- Did the learning and teaching activities help improve the reputation of the service?
- Did the learning and teaching activities help promote our service?

These are questions to ask library and information staff involved in the learning and teaching activities:

- To what extent were the course aims and learning outcomes achieved?
- What worked well and what could be improved?
- How can I improve my training practice with this feedback?

These are questions to ask students:

- To what extent has the learning and teaching activity enhanced my knowledge and skills?
- To what extent has it supported my academic development?
- To what extent has it supported my achievement of my academic goals?
- To what extent has it positively influenced my experiences of the library and information service?

These are questions to ask course leaders and module leaders:

- Did this learning and teaching activity support students on my module or course?
- Did this learning and teaching activity have a positive impact on student achievement?
- What do I need to do to improve the impact of this learning and teaching activity on student achievement?
- Has our money been well spent?
- Did the training event achieve its purpose?

The Kirkpatrick (1959) model is commonly used for evaluating learning and teaching activities. It identifies four levels of evaluation:

- Attitudes or reaction of student: what did they think and feel about the training?
- Learning: what did they learn as a result of the training?
- Behaviour: what impact did the training have on their behaviour, e.g. at work or on their educational course?

- Impact: what was the effect on the library and information service, and the parent organization?

According to more recent research by Alliger and Janak (1989), the relationships between the four levels in this model is weak as each level is not necessarily linked to the next one. This was confirmed by Schilling and Applegate (2012), who found:

- Students' attitudes about the library and librarians may not correlate with their perceptions of their skills and demonstrated skills: there was no correlation between attitude and behaviour.
- Researchers found there is a disconnect between theoretical knowledge and demonstrated skills.

Stevenson (2012) also critiques Kirkpatrick's model in research approaches to evaluation in the context of health service libraries. Stevenson found that the majority of library and information trainers evaluate their training events through reaction (e.g. using 'happy sheets') or learning (diagnostic tests and quizzes or observation). These two measures are the easiest to collect and analyse. The other two measures (behaviour and impact on library and information service) are much more challenging to evaluate and the link between the learning and teaching intervention and change in the library and information service performance may be tenuous. This does not mean it is not worth using these evaluation methods but it can be a challenge!

Despite these criticisms of Kirkpatrick's model it is still well used and provides a relatively simple method for assessing and identifying different approaches to evaluating the impact of learning and teaching activities.

Different methods may be used for different levels of evaluation (attitudes, learning, behaviour and impact) as summarized in Table 10.3 opposite. The different methods are briefly described below, in alphabetical order. Then, there are three case studies showing how researchers have used a combination of tools to evaluate their short courses or training sessions.

Assignments

Academic assignments such as essays, reports, posters and the many other outputs of learning experiences may be used to measure the impact of a course on student achievement. As outlined earlier, it is sometimes challenging for library and information workers to obtain student assessed work and use their work to evaluate their learning.

It should be simpler for library and information workers who are involved in teaching and learning activities that are directly linked to a module or course to have access to student work and the relevant module and course reports. In the

Table 10.3 *Summary of evaluation methods*

Evaluation tools	Attitudes	Learning	Behaviour	Impact
Assignments, e.g. essays, reports, posters		Yes		
Focus groups	Yes			
Interviews	Yes			
Library and information service achievement of key performance indicators				Yes
Library and information service statistics and analytics				Yes
Library and resource usage and analytics			Yes	
Observation	Yes	Yes	Yes	
Portfolios and other products, e.g. learning journals and diaries		Yes		
Practical exercises		Yes		
Surveys	Yes			
Tests		Yes		

UK, the external examiner reports are often helpful, too, and they often comment on students' academic skills, including their information and digital literacies. These comments can provide valuable feedback for their learning and teaching practices.

Focus groups

The concept of focus groups developed in market research. A focus group is a technique to generate qualitative data about a particular product or activity. Typically a small group of six to ten people is brought together to discuss a particular topic, led by one or more facilitators. Focus groups are commonly used in universities so many students are experienced and confident about taking part in them. The real challenge is often getting students to sign up and then attend the event. Sometimes, refreshments and even rewards are used to generate attendance.

Organizing a focus group is likely to involve the following activities:

- identifying the purpose of the focus group; thinking through how it will fit in with other evaluation techniques
- working out the practical arrangements including:
  - timing (remember to check students' timetables to make sure they are available and that it is not close to a hand-in date)
  - venue
  - facilitator(s)
  - identifying potential participants
  - thinking about how to record the feedback, e.g. audio recording, notes
- structuring the focus group:
  - making introductions and welcoming participants
  - explaining the focus group and matters relating to confidentiality
  - giving a small number of trigger questions to start off the discussion

— bringing the discussion to an end and explaining what happens next
— saying thank you and closing the discussion
- obtaining ethics clearance (if required)
- inviting potential participants
- running the focus group
- sending a follow-up thank you e-mail to participants
- reporting the findings.

Interviews

Interviews can be time consuming to organize but very useful as a means of obtaining specific information. Talking to students and their academic staff can be a useful way of obtaining additional feedback about their responses to the course. The practical arrangements for running interviews are similar to those described above for focus groups.

Library and information service achievement of key performance indicators

All library services in colleges and universities are expected to provide annual performance measures, e.g. key performance indicators, some of which may relate to learning and teaching activities. If you are involved in this aspect of library and information services work it is worth spending some time getting to understand the performance measures and how data is collected on learning and teaching activities.

Library and information service statistics and analytics

Libraries and information services are required to demonstrate that they are helping the university or college achieve its strategic aims and outcomes, and this frequently includes being assessed on efficiency and effectiveness measures such as 'value for money'. An extensive range of statistics is collected, e.g. via customer surveys and data analytics from the virtual learning environment, which can be used to demonstrate the impact of learning and teaching courses, e.g. on library use, and use of e-books and e-journals.

Observation

One important approach to observing student learning and behaviour is through observation during a learning and teaching event, when tutors can observe whether or not students:

- use the technical language introduced in the event
- use the search techniques introduced in an information skills session
- ask questions or make comments that indicate they have learnt the required knowledge or skill.

In very small libraries with relatively small numbers of students it is possible to observe students' behaviour, e.g. following a short information literacy course, but for the majority of library and information workers who deal with hundreds or thousands of students this is impractical.

Portfolios and other products

The use of portfolios and other products as part of the assessed work of a module or course raises similar issues to those outlined in the section earlier on assignments. However, library and information workers regularly use a diverse range of products as a means of enabling student learning. These products can help students to work in teams, share their knowledge and experience, and demonstrate their learning to themselves, each other and their tutor. These are some examples of products used by library and information workers in learning activities:

- blogs and wikis
- briefing sheets
- posters, infographs and e-posters
- presentations.

These products may not be formally assessed and so do not contribute to the marks or grades for a particular module or course. Nonetheless, they give tutors a great opportunity to engage students in practical learning activities, and to evaluate their knowledge and skills.

Practical exercises

Practical exercises in all types of learning environments, e.g. face to face and online, provide a relatively simple method of using a learning process, and enable tutors to evaluate the knowledge and behaviours of students. Examples are case studies and hands-on sessions. Students can find it engaging to complete worksheets or produce brief summaries of their learning (using text, audio recording or video recording) and completed exercises provide useful evidence for tutors of what has been learnt and where improvements need to be made.

Surveys

The attitude and reaction of students to a specific learning and teaching activity can be gauged through simple questionnaires or surveys. Typical questions that are asked include:

- Did the event meet your expectations?
- Did you achieve the learning outcomes of the course?
- What did you learn from the event?

- Will the course help you with your current modules and/or assignments?
- What did you like best about the event?
- How could the event be improved?
- Would you recommend this course to another student on your course? If not, please explain why.

However, there are drawbacks to surveys. When assessing very short learning and teaching sessions questionnaires can sometimes appear to be an over-kill, and students receive so many questionnaires and surveys that they are often unwilling to complete another one.

These are some simple and quick methods of collecting feedback from individuals, pairs or small groups using sticky notes, paper, flipcharts or whiteboards:

- The quadrant method: this involves obtaining feedback on a piece of paper or whiteboard that is divided into four sections and then asking the questions shown in Figure 10.1.
- Stop, start, continue: Race (1999) suggests the trainer gives each participant three sticky notes at the start of the session and asks them to write 'stop' on the first, 'start' on the second and 'continue' on the third. As they go through the training event, students complete the sticky notes by recording what they want the trainer to stop doing, start doing, or continue doing. These notes can then be collected at the end of the event (or at an appropriate break).

What did you like about the course?	What did you learn from the course?
What could be improved?	What will you DO as a result of attending this course?

Figure 10.1 *Sample form to complete for the quadrant method of evaluation*

Tests

Tests are commonly used to test knowledge. They are relatively simple to implement given the range of online tools available via most higher education institutions' virtual learning environments or through open software available on the internet. It is worth noting that Schilling and Applegate (2012) found that there was often a disconnect between theoretical knowledge and demonstrated skills. Tests may be used in many different ways including:

- as diagnostic tests before or at the start of a training event
- during a course, e.g. via an audience response system, using the virtual learning environment or paper-based
- at the end of a course, delivered online, using paper or as a group game.

Combined methods of evaluation

Each of the tools outlined above for evaluating learning and teaching activities are useful for specific purposes and have their own advantages and disadvantages. As a result, it is normal practice to combine a number of different methods so as to provide a more robust evaluation process. This is demonstrated in the following case studies.

Case study: Does it improve the marks?

Edwards and Hill (2012) described their approach to evaluating the impact of an information literacy workshop on the marks of second year undergraduate computer science students. They used a survey and correlated the findings with the students' marks for their assessed work. They found that students who attended a two-hour training session gained higher marks than students who did not attend. The most frequently occurring mark for students who attended the session was 65% (50% for non-attenders), and the highest mark for student attenders was 90% (75% for non-attenders). The attenders' bibliography marks were higher too (7/10 compared with 5/10 for non-attenders). Edwards and Hill considered the challenges of attempting to measure the impact of training sessions on student performance and note that a significant number of students did not take advantage of the training session.

Case study: The impact of library information literacy classes on first-year undergraduate students' search behaviour

Boger et al. (2015) used a combination of interviews and observation to measure the impact of information literacy sessions on first-year undergraduate students' behaviour. Their research involved students who had attended the sessions as well as those who did not attend. They summarize their findings as follows:

The aim of this study was to investigate how the first year students at Østfold University College describe their search for information and how information literacy classes influence their searching behaviour. Through the interviews and observation conducted, only slight differences between the students, who attended the IL training and those who did not, have been found.

Some of the students that had attended the course mentioned that they would use the library services and resources in the future, but apart from this, the responses from the two groups did not differ much. The first year students lack understanding of what is expected from them when entering higher education. They need to be taught and motivated to use relevant academic skills, such as information searching.

(Boger et al., 2015, 43–4)

Case study: Snakes or ladders?

Dalton and Rosalind (2014) give an outline of the project management process involved in implementing a LibGuides pilot at the library of University College Dublin (UCD). LibGuides, a cloud-based product, provides a dynamic approach to supporting learners with numerous resources and technologies, including social media. It is a relatively simple approach to supporting new undergraduate students and guiding them through the vast range of available information and resources.

Dalton and Rosalind describe the project management process for the following work packages:

- work package 1: preparation
- work package 2: full investigation of LibGuides options and finalization of format
- work package 3: building the pilot sets of LibGuides
- work package 4: management systems
- work package 5: promotional strategy to support live roll-out of pilot pages
- work package 6: evaluation and review of pilot.

The evaluation process (work package 6) is explored in this case study. It involved two strands:

- quantitative usage statistics and analytics
- qualitative feedback from students, academic staff and library staff.

Quantitative usage data was collected using the built-in statistics from the product augmented using Google Analytics, which enabled the team to track the origin of users (UCD, Ireland, beyond). They found that usage of the LibGuides varied among the student population and that without access to student population data it was difficult to compare usage.

Qualitative data was collected in various ways including through:

- informal feedback from communications with academic staff
- informal feedback from meetings with academic staff
- library staff feedback
- student feedback (considered vital to the project) collected via a pop-up feedback stand during a busy mid-morning period; two liaison librarians asked students to complete a three-question survey and answer the following questions:
  — Had they heard of or used the guides?
  — How would they rate the guide on a scale of 1–10?
  — What feature did they find most helpful or would like to be added to the guides?

The results from the quantitative and qualitative data were then used to inform the next stage of the project.

For further information see Dalton and Rosalind (2014).

Summary

Library and information workers involved in supporting student learning need to be knowledgeable about their institution's approach to quality assurance and enhancement. This will enable them to engage with these processes and develop their learning and teaching activities.

Many library and information service activities that relate to students' learning and achievements are not formally evaluated as part of the institutional processes. In this situation, a library and information service policy and process for the evaluation of the library's short courses, training sessions and online courses will provide evidence which may be used to demonstrate their impact and improve the quality of this provision.

This chapter gives a summary of many of the popular evaluation tools and techniques, and case studies that demonstrate the use of a combination of tools used to evaluate learning and teaching activities.

References

Alliger, G. and Janak, E. (1989) Kirkpatrick's Levels of Training Criteria: thirty years later, *Personnel Psychology*, **42** (2), 331–42.

Boger, T. S., Dybvik, H., Eng, A. and Norheim, E. H. (2015) The Impact of Library Information Literacy Classes on First-year Undergraduate Students' Search Behaviour, *Journal of Information Literacy*, **9** (1), 34–46.

Dalton, M. and Rosalind, P. (2014) Snakes or Ladders? Evaluating a LibGuides pilot at University College Dublin Library, *Journal of Academic Librarianship*, forthcoming, http://researchrepository.ucd.ie.

Edwards, A. and Hill, V. (2012) Does it Really Improve Their Marks?, *SCONUL Focus*, **56**, 27–9.

Kirkpatrick, D. L. (1959) Techniques for Evaluating Training Programs, *Journal of the American Society of Training and Development*, **33** (11), 3–9.

QAA (2014a) *UK Quality Code for Higher Education*, www.qaa.ac.uk/assuring-standards-and-quality/the-quality-code.

QAA (2014b) *What Students Think of their Higher Education: analysis of student submissions to the Quality Assurance Agency for Higher Education in 2012–13*, www.qaa.ac.uk/en/Publications/Documents/What-Students-Think-of-Their-Higher-Education.pdf.

Race, P. (1999) *2000 Tips for Lecturers*, Kogan Page.

Schilling, K. and Applegate, R. (2012) Best Methods for Evaluating Educational Impact: a comparison of the efficacy of commonly used measures of library instruction, *Journal of the Medical Library Association*, **100** (4), 258–70.

Stevenson, P. (2012) Evaluating Educational Interventions for Information Literacy, *Health Information & Libraries Journal*, **29** (1), 81–6.

11

Lifelong professional development

Introduction

Chapter 1 outlined how rapid developments affecting higher education are changing the ways in which library and information workers support students' learning and achievement. The need to maintain and update professional knowledge and skills is vital in order to continue to develop and innovate library and information services and resources, so that they meet the needs of their stakeholders.

This chapter explores different approaches to keeping up to date and developing one's professional profile. It starts by outlining the range of learning and development opportunities available to library and information workers. Many are available in the workplace, through professional organizations and education providers, as well as through independent activities, e.g. social networking. These are considered under the following themes: networking through professional organizations; learning in the workplace; short courses, conferences and workshops; accredited courses; independent learning; and developing online networks. In practice, there is much overlap between these different approaches to keeping up to date. The final sections are concerned with managing individual professional development (short term immediate needs and longer term career planning) and developing a portfolio.

Networking through professional organizations and groups

An important method of keeping up to date and gaining support is through local, regional, national or international library and information professional networks. Professional associations such as the Chartered Institute for Library and Information Professionals (CILIP) in the UK, the American Library Association (ALA) and the Australian Library and Information Association (ALIA) offer a range of services to members, which typically include: giving access to professional journals and other resources; giving access to specialist events, workshops and conferences; professional accreditation; discounted fees for books and events; and other benefits.

Professional associations are likely to provide information, support and guidance for all stages of a career, from advice about professional accredited courses through to support and guidance for senior staff. Their websites give access to a vast array of information and resources, as demonstrated by the following examples.

Example: The American Library Association

The American Library Association (ALA; www.ala.org) provides an extensive variety of membership benefits including the option for individual library and information workers who do not hold US citizenship and are not employed in the USA to be international members. Members have access to many resources and learning opportunities, e.g. through conferences and webinars, as well as online toolkits and a tools portal.

Specialist groups include the ACRL (www.ala.org/acrl/), whose website gives access to many resources, including:

- guidelines, standards and frameworks such as the *Framework for Information Literacy for Higher Education* (2014), available in English and Chinese
- online learning – courses, live webcasts, webinars and webcasts
- the TechConnect blog, which provides access to up-to-date information about technology and its applications in academic libraries
- communications and discussion areas such as ACRL Insider, ACRLog, ACRL OnPoint Chat, ALA Connect and ACRL Wiki
- e-mail updates and discussion lists
- toolkits on themes such as the value of academic libraries, advocacy, information literacy competency standards, marketing and scholarly communication.

Example: The Chartered Institute for Library and Information Professionals

Members of the Chartered Institute for Library and Information Professionals (CILIP; www.cilip.org.uk) have access to an online-membership-only site, which contains:

- information about CILIP and its networks and special interest groups
- information on advocacy, campaigns and awards
- information on jobs and careers: jobs from Lisjobnet, the Professional Knowledge and Skills Base, professional registration
- information on membership
- news and blogs
- information on events
- information on products and services.

Within CILIP, specific groups are particularly helpful for anyone working in higher education including:

- the Academic and Research Libraries Group (ARLG)
- the Information Literacy Group (ILG).

Some groups such as the ILG have their own extensive website (see www.informationliteracy. org.uk/). The ILG organizes the annual Librarians' Information Literacy Annual Conference (LILAC), which is described later in this chapter. Many special groups keep in touch with their members via websites and social media.

Example: The Hong Kong Library Association

The website of the Hong Kong Library Association (HKLA; www.hkla.org) is in two Chinese languages as well as English. It provides access to information on an extensive range of library and information studies courses from short ones through to master's degrees in Hong Kong and overseas. It also gives information on conferences and other events, and access to job vacancies.

Example: The Indian Library Association

The Indian Library Association (ILA; www.ilaindia.net/) website gives access in English to an e-news bulletin and a peer-reviewed e-journal. The LIS gateway provides links to guides and tutorials, information on information literacy and virtual tours, and has a list of libraries and projects throughout the world. This resource is valuable to anyone wanting to explore library and information services and resources internationally.

Learning in the workplace

Allan (2013) identified more than 90 approaches to learning and teaching in the workplace. An updated list is presented in Figure 11.1 on the next page. The key message from this list is that virtually everything that happens in the library or information service or wider community provides opportunities for learning and development.

Another important development is that students are often now considered to be co-creators within higher education institutions (see Chapter 5) and are embedded in the work of the library and they may be involved in staff development activities. Many libraries engage students in their staff development conferences and workshops; some employ them as roving digital guides to provide support to library and information workers and their peers; others employ them as interns, and use this as an opportunity for finding out about students' expectations and ways of working (see Chapter 4).

Short courses, conferences and workshops

Short courses, conferences and workshops all provide great opportunities for learning and development as a participant, presenter or facilitator. They may be delivered face to face or through e-learning, e.g. via a webinar or massive online

360 degree feedback	Exhibitions	Presentations
	Exit interviews	Professional journals
Accreditations	External funding	Professional organizations
Action learning	External projects	Project work
Action planning		Promotion
Analysing mistakes	Feedback	
Appraisal processes	Fishbone diagram	Quality assurance activities
Apps	Focus groups	Quizzes
Asking advice	Frequently asked questions	
Asking and answering questions		Reading
Audio recordings	Gap year	Reflection
		Retreats or residentials
Benchmarking	Induction	Rich pictures
Blogs	Instructions	
Book reviews	Internet	Secondment
Briefing papers	Interviews	Self-assessment tools
Briefing sessions		Setting deadlines
	Job rotation	Social media
Cascade training		Speed networking
Celebrating success	Key performance indicators	Stakeholders
Coaching	Learning boxes	Sticky notes
Communities of interest and	Learning contracts	Students
practice	Learning conversations	Study tours
Competitions and prizes	Learning journals	SWOT analysis
Complaints		
Conferences	Mailing lists	Teamwork
Covering for holidays	Meetings	Training a colleague
Crises	Mentoring	Twitter
Critical friends	Metaphors	
	Mind Mapping™	Video clips
Delegation		Visits
Demonstrations	Networking	
Displays		Wikis
	Online discussion groups	Work-based learning
E-bulletins and e-journals	Online tutorials	qualifications
E-learning	Organizing events	Work shadowing
E-mails		Working parties
E-portfolio	Personal development planning	Writing
Evaluating different products	Personal development portfolios	
Exchanges	Playing cards	YouTube

Figure 11.1 *Approaches to learning in the workplace (Allan 2013)*

open course (MOOC). It can be a challenge to identify an appropriate event as there are so many providers, including:

- universities and colleges
- professional bodies
- professional groups and networks
- private suppliers.

Short courses and workshops are particularly useful for:

- updating knowledge and skills
- gaining new knowledge and skills
- meeting colleagues who may be grappling with similar workplace issues.

MOOCs offer access to free online courses available from many universities and providers such as Coursera and FutureLearn. They may be used for personal development for a number of reasons, including to:

- update knowledge and skills
- develop knowledge about specific disciplines
- learn about the design and delivery of online courses.

Library and information professional associations across the world offer access to free (to members and sometimes the public) and pay to view courses. Websites of organizations such as ALA (the American Library Association), ALIA (the Australian Library and Information Association), CILIP: the Chartered Institute of Library and Information Professionals and LIANZA (the Library and Information Association of New Zealand) indicate that these organizations provide a wide range of online courses, giving opportunities for learning in the workplace, at home or while travelling. Taking part in an online course hosted in a different country can provide exciting opportunities for networking and learning about very different points of view.

Case study: Bridging the mobile gap

Munro and Stevenson (2013) describe how they developed a staff development programme to support library and information services staff in their development of digital skills. The blog '23 Things' developed by the Public Library of Charlotte and Mecklenburg County sparked the idea of concentrating on 23 discrete aspects of mobile technology. They grouped the content into the following themes:

- devices phones, tablets
- networks wifi, 3G or 4G, the cloud
- applications mobile web, apps, QR code
- communicating blogs, text or instant messaging, e-mail, Facebook, Twitter
- library stuff: e-books, e-journals, mobile databases
- fun stuff: Live Lab, music, photos or videos, gaming
- other mobile futures, 23 Things quiz.

The programme was managed via the library's virtual learning environment (Moodle), a blog and live hands-on sessions.

Case study: LibTalks

Wallis and Gerrard (2014) write about the development of LibTalks as a means of enabling innovation, learning and development within their information services team. They describe the challenges to staff development including time and money (e.g. to attend events outside the university). The LibTalks were face-to-face events; over the academic year eight guest speakers (six of them from other universities) came and led a talk in an informal semi-structured setting with tea and coffee. The purpose was to discuss innovation, to share ideas and to promote discussions and debates. They write about how each session was run and their use of social media:

> *The person who organised the session also chaired and led the discussion, supported by the other two members of the group; one as designated 'tweeter' and one as notetaker. The presentations are then put up on an internal SharePoint site with the accompanying notes for anyone who was unable to attend. Due to the popularity and word-of-mouth publicity, we attracted high levels of external attendees, which led us to start a publicly accessible blog.*
>
> (Wallis and Gerrard, 2014, 54)

Conferences provide a means for wider networking and learning from peers. They vary hugely in the costs and time commitment involved; online conferences offer an alternative to traditional conferences. In order to make the most of conferences it is worthwhile to:

- become involved in their organization, e.g. as a committee member or volunteer
- submit a paper or poster
- offer to run a workshop
- use social media, e.g. write a conference blog or tweet (see later in this chapter)
- read all the advance information and identify people you wish to contact; contact them via social media prior to the conference
- network while you are there
- write a summary of your experience, e.g. for colleagues, an in-house e-bulletin or a professional journal.

Increasingly, conference presentations, blogs and other resources become available on their organizing bodies website after the event providing even wider access to the ideas explored in the conference.

Example: The Librarians' Information Literacy Annual Conference

The annual Librarians' Information Literacy Annual Conference (LILAC; www.lilacconference.com/) is organized by CILIP's ILG and is aimed at librarians and information professionals involved in information literacy and digital literacies. It is an international conference and typically delegates come from more than 30 countries. The conference encourages library and information professionals at all stages of their career, including students via sponsorship.

The LILAC archive website provides access to presentations going back to 2011 (see http://archive.lilacconference.com/). LILAC is a very active and engaging conference with sites on Facebook and LinkedIn, as well as a Twitter stream.

Accredited courses

Formal accredited courses are often a useful approach to career development and lead to academic and/or professional qualifications. The following course subjects are likely to be of interest to individuals supporting student learning:

- library and information studies
- learning and teaching in higher education
- digital media and/or digital marketing
- project management.

Accredited courses in library and information studies involve full- or part-time undergraduate or postgraduate study taught face to face, or through distance teaching, online learning or blended learning. More information about accredited courses is available from professional associations such as ALA, ALIA and CILIP.

There are many different ways of learning about educational practices, from individual modules to full degree programmes. In addition, it may be possible to gain professional accreditation by developing a portfolio and submitting it to the accrediting body (or local institution if it has been accredited for this type of award). Many universities and colleges provide their own in-house education programmes or let their staff go on courses elsewhere. Typical courses are postgraduate certificates in higher education or a master's degree in education. In the UK, these courses are likely to be accredited by the Higher Education Academy (www.heacademy.ac.uk). Likewise other countries have their own accreditation schemes for learning and teaching in higher education.

Throughout this book, it has been demonstrated that digital skills are essential for supporting student learning. Many people have developed their digital skills on the job and through short courses and workshops, and it is possible to gain qualifications in this area. A number of universities and colleges now offer part-time master's degrees in digital media and digital skills. In addition, professional groups such as marketing organizations have developed a number of practical-skills-based courses, for example:

- the Institute of Direct and Digital Marketing (www.theidm.com/qualifications/)
- the Marketers' Forum (www.themarketersforum.co.uk/).

Project management skills and techniques are widely used in libraries and information services and it is possible to obtain qualifications and professional accreditation in project management too. Many universities and colleges offer accredited short courses in project management (often scheduled over three to five days or as an evening course), for example:

- PRINCE2®: Foundation
- PRINCE2®: Practitioner
- PRINCE2®: Foundation and Practitioner
- AgilePM®: Agile Project Management™ Certification – Foundation
- AgilePM®: Agile Project Management™ Certification – Foundation and Practitioner
- AgilePM®: Agile Project Management™ Certification – Practitioner
- M_o_R® Certification: Management of Risk
- MSP®: Managing Successful Programmes Certification.

Commercial training providers also run these types of short course. Many library and information services use formal project management tools and techniques for small and large complex projects. Gaining a project management qualification is a valuable addition to anyone's CV and the knowledge gained from a project management course can be useful in the workplace.

Independent learning

In addition to MOOCs and other online courses, an extensive range of learning resources support individual learning and development. The challenge is to identify and evaluate appropriate resources as this can be very time consuming.

Keeping up to date with the professional literature, e.g. journals and bulletins from professional associations, peer-reviewed journals in library and information studies, learning and teaching, and technology enhanced learning, can be a real challenge. One time-saving approach is to work with colleagues and/or networks and for individuals to take responsibility for providing briefing notes and an alerting service on specific publications or organizations. Following some active professionals blogs (see 'Blogging' on page 163) can also be a useful short cut to keeping up to date.

The following case study and examples demonstrate the resources that are available from various organizations.

Case study: Learning from guides and tool kits

Jisc (see www.jisc.ac.uk) produces an excellent set of well written and accessible guides and resources on a vast range of subjects related to technology enhanced learning and teaching. Jisc guides cover all stages in the use of digital media in the learning and teaching process, including on topics such as making a video. Their InfoKits cover topics such as:

- games
- gamification

- enhancing presentations using digital media
- use of microphones.

Jisc also runs workshops, webinars and other development events.

Example: Learning resources from professional associations
These are some of the learning resources from professional associations:

- The Council of Australian University Librarians (CAUL; www.caul.edu.au) has many publications on subjects such as information literacy.
- The Higher Education Academy (HEA; https://www.heacademy.ac.uk/) has an extensive range of resources and reports relating to current themes and issues in higher education.
- The Indian Library Association (ILA; www.ilaindia.net/) provides access to an LIS gateway (www.ilaindia.net/LIS-Gateway.htm), which has an extensive resources bibliography and gives access and links on topics such as guides and tutorials, information literacy and virtual tours.
- The Library and Information Association of New Zealand (LIANZA; www.lianza.org.nz/) provides access to an extensive variety of learning resources at www.lianza.org.nz/learning-resources. These include articles, presentations and talks on topics such as project management and starting to blog.
- The Society of College, National and University Libraries (SCONUL; http://sconul.ac.uk) gives access to a range of publications and reports including *SCONUL Focus*, which has relatively short and very readable articles on current practice.

Developing online networks
Networking enables one to meet other professionals working in library and information services, and individuals in other networks of interest such as learning and teaching, e-learning, marketing or project management. Through networking it is possible to discuss and pick up new ideas, obtain feedback on current issues, look for employment, and gain advice and support. As mentioned earlier in this chapter, many professional library and information associations provide access to their online groups and networks.

Online networking involves spending time creating and maintaining an online identity. This is a relatively simple process during which individuals develop a personal profile for sites of their employer, professional association and social media such as LinkedIn or Facebook. Many library and information professionals also use tools such as Twitter, Facebook, LinkedIn, Flickr, a blogging tool and/or YouTube. It is up to individuals (and their employing organization) to determine the range of social media to be used. Note that more value may be gained from using a small number of tools well rather than many tools intermittently.

The constant development of new social media tools and the rise and fall of the use of specific tools as trends change makes this is an area of activity that is constantly evolving and changing. Consequently, individuals need to keep up to date with online trends and then decide whether or not to engage with new tools, and when to drop the use of some media.

This section is concerned with the following topics:

- using LinkedIn and equivalent sites
- blogging
- Twitter
- Instagram
- Pinterest.

It is important for library or information workers to read and follow their institution's policies and guidelines for the use of social media before starting to use them for professional reasons. Line managers can provide guidance if required.

Using LinkedIn and equivalent sites

Sites such as LinkedIn and Facebook are useful for networking, exchanging information and ideas, and job hunting. A quick search on Facebook using the term 'information literacy' results in more than 50 sites from around the world – from America to Sri Lanka. These include open and closed groups, groups associated with specific universities and colleges, and those linked to specific information literacy conferences. The same search on LinkedIn produced a similar set of international groups. It is worth noting that access to social media varies across the world so it cannot be assumed that all library and information professionals in all countries have access to them.

Using a social media site such as LinkedIn or Facebook has two stages: creating an online profile and then maintaining it. It is helpful to prepare the relevant information and resources before uploading it. Typically the following information is required about the person involved:

- name and job title
- a professional headline – a 5–10 key word summary identifying experience and expertise
- a personal URL
- location and sector, e.g. higher education, further education
- a photograph – normally a headshot
- a personal summary outlining expertise and areas of interest, and professional history
- experience: current role
- experience: past roles

- skills: a list of 10–15 skills
- education: include academic and professional qualifications
- awards: any award or other special achievement.

Different social media sites offer different options for inputting personal information and they continue to expand their range of options. Individuals need to decide how much or how little to include on the site. Once the information is uploaded it needs to be checked before it is published online. Many people ask a colleague or friend to check their site. Once it is 100% correct then it can be published.

Online networking involves as little or as much time as an individual wishes to spend on the activity. Some people seem to be active on an hourly basis; others go online once a day, every few days, or once a week. Different ways of being active online include:

- expanding your network by making connections with other people
- liking and sharing other people's or organization's content
- joining relevant online groups and contributing to their discussions
- uploading your own content, e.g. news of new projects, resources, activities
- using the recommendations tool (if available).

Blogging

Blogging provides a simple approach to putting a message across to other library and information workers, students or colleagues. The discipline of writing a regular blog and the research required to support it makes it a form of professional development. There are different tools for blogging including use of a home institution's technology or one of the many freely available blogging tools such as WordPress or Blogger, or those available through LinkedIn. It is relatively easy to create a blog but keeping it going requires discipline and a regular time commitment, e.g. an hour or two each week or month.

These are some general guidelines for writing a blog:

- Start with an enticing sentence.
- Use a conversational and friendly tone: imagine that it will be read by a friend.
- Keep it simple: avoid technical jargon and explain any acronyms.
- Keep it short: 50–250 words.
- Use photographs or images to break up your text.

Example: Personal selection of blogs

These are some blogs that I follow:

- Information Literacy Weblog (http://information-literacy.blogspot.co.uk)
- Phil Bradley's Weblog (www.philbradley.typepad.com)
- In the Library with the Lead Pipe (www.inthelibrarywiththeleadpipe.org)
- Mr. Library Dude (https://mrlibrarydude.wordpress.com/)
- Educause (www.educause.edu).

Twitter

Twitter is an information network, which can provide access to very current information and news from individuals, organizations, conferences, projects and other Twitter account holders. It is a form of micro-blogging. It is increasingly standard practice for library and information services to have their own Twitter account and individuals often use them for professional purposes.

It is very simple to set up a personal or library Twitter account. Go to http://twitter.com and give a personal Twitter name and a brief description, either personal or of your service or project. Accounts can be personalized to meet individual or library needs. Twitter provides a very useful help centre, which gives clear advice on getting the best out of this tool. Most people connect to Twitter via an app on their mobile phone and this gives a very simple and convenient approach to keeping up to date.

Getting going with Twitter involves:

- finding and following other users
- sending tweets (short messages of no more than 140 characters)
- responding to other people's tweets
- forwarding tweets.

Instagram

Instagram is a simple way of sharing photos or very short videos. It is simple to set up an account (go to https://instagram.com). Using Instagram it is possible to share photos and videos on social networking platforms such as Facebook, LinkedIn, Twitter, Tumblr and Flickr. Mollett and McDonnell (2014) present a summary of some of the ways in which they use Instagrams, including:

- to show off their library and collections
- to publicize events
- to show behind the scenes of the library and information service
- to show their library history and heritage.

Pinterest

Pinterest (https://uk.pinterest.com) is an online visual tool used to save and display images, videos and other resources (known as pins – a visual bookmark) in one place (the pin board); it can be accessed via the web and through apps.

Pinterest accounts may be linked to other social media, e.g. Facebook and LinkedIn.

An example of a university library Pinterest account can be seen at https://uk.pinterest.com/hullunilibrary/around-the-library. The University of Albany libraries use Pinterest as a means for sharing events, tips and their collections (see UAlbany Libraries Pinterest boards).The University of Texas at Austin has written a useful guide on Pinterest, which is available at http://guides.lib.utexas.edu. Individual library and information workers use Pinterest to present a visual overview of their work and projects. Ward Sell (2014) provides an interesting article on Pinterest, suggesting that it may be used to encourage interest and engagement with students and other library users.

Managing individual professional development

The previous sections described various development opportunities for library and information workers under the following headings:

- networking through professional organizations
- learning in the workplace
- short courses, conferences and workshops
- accredited courses
- independent learning
- developing online networks.

Using these themes helps to organize different learning and development opportunities, but there is much overlap between them as illustrated in the following example.

Example: An academic librarian's development activities

Sarah, a liaison librarian, joined the professional association CILIP and used it to update herself through the association's online resources and toolkits, and by attending conferences. She made contact with other liaison librarians at an information literacy workshop and they established a group on Facebook, which was live for about nine months. Her enthusiasm for social media grew and she followed a webinar on the use of social media for beginners. When attending a national conference Sarah tweeted throughout; then she enthusiastically decided to start her own blog. However, she wanted to know more about blogging and knew that one of the students in her faculty was a well known blogger. She asked her for advice and the student gave her an informal coaching session to get her going. Six months later, Sarah updates her blog about every three weeks and has been asked to co-deliver a session on blogging to her colleagues.

In this example, Sarah followed her own interests and enthusiasms in an organic style. Many people find it useful to take a more structured approach to their development and this may take place at two levels: by looking at one's immediate professional needs and by assessing one's long-term career goals.

Immediate professional needs

The rapidly changing landscape in higher education, as outlined in Chapter 1, has resulted in an increased drive for professional development in order to meet the needs of current students (and their potential employers). Immediate professional needs may be identified as a result of changes to the service and professional role, changes in the structure and organization of the library and information service, personal awareness of a gap in knowledge and skills, or feedback from colleagues or other stakeholders.

One source of help when listing immediate development needs is through frameworks that set out the knowledge and skills required for a profession, as produced by organizations such as CILIP and ALA. These are often associated with self-assessment tools to enable individuals to recognize their strengths and development needs. Another source of guidance is the tools used within universities or colleges. Diagnostic tools and frameworks, e.g. graduate attributes, are often used to help guide students on their development needs. Using these tools has a double benefit as they enable individuals to discover their training and development needs, and to gain an insight into students' experiences as they work through the same diagnostic and reflective processes.

Immediate professional needs are commonly discussed and agreed with the library worker's manager. Meeting these needs may involve developing and agreeing a learning contract such as the one shown in Figure 11.2.

Name	
Overall aim of professional development plan	
Link to Library and Information Service strategic and operational plans	
Intended learning outcome(s)	
Method(s) of learning and development, e.g. coaching, online course	
Indicative time and timing of development activities	
Indicative cost	
Date of completion	
Method(s) of dissemination to colleagues	
Signature:	Date:
Manager signature:	Date:

Figure 11.2 *Sample learning contract*

Long-term career goals

Aligning immediate professional needs with long-term career goals is sensible so library and information workers know their goals and understand how their short term development activities fit into their longer term plan. A useful starting point for any library or information worker is to identify their personal goals and what is important to them. This may take place through a formal process led by library managers and supervisors such as an annual personal and professional development or appraisal process. Alternatively, individuals may choose to manage their careers themselves by reflecting on questions such as:

- Where am I now in my career?
- What aspects of my work do I enjoy and would like to develop further?
- What aspects of my work do I not enjoy and want to move away from?
- Is there anything different that I want to do, e.g. change my work–life balance, travel, volunteer?
- Where do I want to be in three years' time and five years' time?

As part of this process, many library and information workers find it helpful to complete a professional knowledge and skills inventory, which may be available from their own institution or from professional associations such as ALA, ALIA and CILIP. This review process helps individuals to consider their professional profile, its strengths and areas for development.

There are many books which provide this type of help and guidance, such as *What Color is your Parachute?* (Bolles, 2015).

Developing a professional portfolio

A professional portfolio is valuable to track immediate professional activities and development, and for long-term career development. A portfolio is also useful for anyone working in higher education, where students are commonly involved in developing their portfolios for future employers, to understand the processes that they are going through, as this helps to provide more specialist support.

A portfolio is an electronic or paper-based record of personal information that contains the following types of information:

- a curriculum vitae
- personal statement(s)
- an assessment of strengths and weaknesses, e.g. against a competency framework
- development plan(s)
- supporting statements, e.g. from managers, colleagues, customers
- records of learning activities, e.g. training attended, qualifications
- examples of products, e.g. library guides, articles, newsletters, blogs, video clips.

Many universities, colleges and professional bodies provide access to an e-portfolio for their staff or members. The advantages of using an e-portfolio over a paper-based one is that it enables an individual to organize, display and manage work in a wide range of formats, e.g. with Word or PDF files, PowerPoint presentations, audio or video files, graphics and other multimedia. It is relatively easy to publish, archive or share an e-portfolio. Developing a personal portfolio and reviewing it at regular intervals, e.g. monthly or three monthly, provides a means of capturing valuable information, which may be used for career progression.

Professional portfolios may be used in a number of different ways including:

- when applying for a new position
- when applying for a professional qualification
- to help boost self-esteem.

Case study: The CILIP portfolio system

CILIP provides an e-portfolio system with social networking features to create online learning communities. It is available to members and enables individuals to:

- create and collect: upload their profile, create a CV, upload files and publish a journal
- organize: create different pages for different audiences
- share and network using social media.

CILIP has many workshops to help individuals develop their portfolio in preparation for professional recognition. Members can share them online (see Bethan's Information Professional Blog at https://bethaninfoprof.wordpress.com).
A useful resource is *Building your Portfolio* (Own and Watson, 2015).

Summary

It can be challenging and time consuming to keep up to date in the changing context of higher education and, in particular, the rapid developments in technologies that support learning and teaching. Fortunately, the rapid availability of different technologies including social media makes it relatively easy to keep in touch with development using a variety of mobile tools such as phones, tablets and laptops.

This chapter demonstrates the many different ways in which it is possible to keep abreast of professional knowledge and skills. There are many face-to-face and online learning activities to choose from. Professional development can be enhanced by working with students in the library, e.g. through work placements, or through other activities. Finally, this chapter considers planning and organizing individuals' immediate professional development needs and long-term career goals, which may include developing a portfolio.

References

Allan, B. (2013) *The No-Nonsense Guide to Training*, Facet Publishing.

Bolles, R. N. (2015) *What Color is your Parachute?: a practical manual for job-hunters and career-changers*, Penguin Random House.

Mollett, A. and McDonnell, A. (2014) Five Ways Libraries Are Using Instagram to Share Collections and Draw Public Interest, blog, http:// blogs.lse.ac.uk.

Munro, K. and Stevenson, K. (2013) Bridging the Mobile Skills Gap for Library Staff, *SCONUL Focus*, **58**, 16–19.

Owen, K. and Watson, M. (2015) *Building your Portfolio*, Facet Publishing.

Wallis, K. and Gerrard, K. (2014) Innovation Through Discussion: the LibChats initiative at the University of Kent, *SCONUL Focus*, **61**, 51–5.

Ward Sell, C. (2014) Pinning it Down, *SCONUL Focus*, **62**, 37–41.

Index